His Leadership Her Trust

4 Steps to Become the Christian Man
A Woman Trusts, Respects, and *Actually* Wants to
Follow

By

Heath Wiggins

Published by Best Seller Publishing®, Pasadena, CA
Best Seller Publishing® is a registered trademark
Printed in the United States of America.
ISBN-13: 978-1511945974
ISBN-10: 1511945974

This publication is designed to provide accurate and authoritative
information with regard to the subject matter covered. It is sold
with the understanding that the publisher is not engaged in
rendering legal, accounting, or other professional advice. If legal
advice or other expert assistance is required, the services of a
competent professional should be sought. The opinions
expressed by the authors in this book are not endorsed by Best
Seller Publishing® and are the sole responsibility of the author
rendering the opinion.

Most Best Seller Publishing® titles are available at special
quantity discounts for bulk purchases for sales promotions,
premiums, fundraising, and educational use. Special versions or
book excerpts can also be created to fit specific needs.

For more information, please write:
Best Seller Publishing®
1346 Walnut Street, #205
Pasadena, CA 91106
or call 1(626) 765 9750
Toll Free: 1(844) 850-3500
Visit us online at: www.BestSellerPublishing.org

Table of Contents

Preface: The Cheat Sheet

The Four Steps

Some people, like me, don't want to have to read an entire book to get the lesson I'm supposed to receive. You want to skip right to the bottom line. So I've created this cheat sheet up front that tells you the four steps to be the man a woman trusts, respects, and actually wants to follow, known as the I.C.E.C Leadership Model.

When you have a goal you want to accomplish in your relationship, follow these four steps:

Step 1. **Initiate**: Initiate the roles regarding who is responsible for what tasks.

Step 2. **Communicate**: Communicate the goal you want to accomplish to your mate and wait for her feedback.

Step 3. **Execut**e: Execute your judgment/decision.

Step 4. **Check-in**: Check in with your mate throughout the execution of your judgment/decision.

Little Known Secrets This Book Also Uncovers...

Early in my marriage to my wife BerNadette, I realized I needed to be a better leader because I was struggling trying to figure out how to lead my family in the direction we wanted to go. I needed someone to clearly explain to me what leadership is and how to translate that information into being a better leader in my marriage. So I invested in my education and spent the next 10 years researching answers to those questions.

In discovering these four steps, I also uncovered little known secrets about relationships that can increase a man's level of trust and respect to the point where a woman actually wants to follow him. The secrets this book reveals are:

- What *leadership* is and what it is not

- *When* to provide leadership in your relationship and when your leadership is nullified

- The *three goals* God gave every married couple and how to implement them

- What God's *test taking process* is and how it develops you as a leader

- What the *process of influence* is, which is the key to leadership

- What *power* is, and how to properly use *power resources* to lead

- How your *value system* influences what you believe is truth and reality

- What *persuasion* is, and how to successfully convince your mate to change her mind and go with your suggestion

- How to use your *intuition* and *judgment* to make decisions

- The difference between a *novice* and *expert decision maker*, and how to make decisions like an expert in your relationship

Without a clear understanding of these elements and how they are integrated with the four steps, you won't unpack the full potential of your leadership.

This book is divided into two parts. Part 1 is informational and Part 2 is instructional. In Part 1, *What Leadership in Relationships Look Like*, I identify the two types of relationship structures. Based on which relational structure you're in determines whether you can even be a leader. I define what leadership is, how it works in relationships, and how it doesn't work in relationships. I also discuss how God prepares you for leadership.

In Part 2, *Four Steps to Providing Leadership in Your Relationships—Initiate, Communicate, Execute, and Check-in*, I break down the definition of leadership into easy to understand steps you can do in your relationship.

If you skip Part 1 and go straight to Part 2, you won't understand why you're doing the four steps. If you read Part 1 and never read Part 2, you'll understand what you need to do to be a leader, but you won't know *how* to do it. Take your time and read carefully through both parts. This is not a sprint. Pace yourself. The more you understand both parts, the better leader you will become.

Need help obtaining or maintaining leadership in your relationship? JOIN our men only online community for leaders in relationships and receive FREE awesome content: www.HisLeadershipHerTrust.com/thebook.

Introduction:
Increase in Divorce After WW II

When our soldiers landed at the naval and air force bases around the country in the mid-1940s, the United States was reveling in its World War II victory. These heroic men were greeted with great fanfare, parades, and celebrations for their selfless service to their country.

But when they came back home from war, they were met with a completely different domestic landscape.

When American men went to war, it caused a serious labor shortage in the country. Women, who traditionally worked in the home, were now taking on the jobs once reserved for men in the industrial factories. These dual-dutied women had to assume the role of working full-time and taking care of all the responsibilities at home.

The burden on families during World War II was no different than previous wars; divorces slightly ticked up during the war and after it ended. Prior to WW II, if a woman wanted to get a divorce, she had to have a job that took care of herself and her children. If she didn't have the means, she'd have to stay and suffer through it until her fortunes turned around, if they ever did.

When the men returned to their civilian lives, the women were now a mainstay in the workforce. Some women stayed on because their husband or father didn't make it back home. But others stayed on to increase financial security for the family. Post-war women now had options. If a wife didn't like the way her husband was behaving or leading the family, she now had the option to leave and take care of the family on her own. And leave she did.

During World War II, between 1941 and 1944, divorces increased more sharply than ever before: 0.9% in 1941 to 1.8% in 1944.[1] In the 1950s, the divorce rate steadily rose from 1.0% in 1950, topping out at 2.3% in 1979. [2] In the decades that followed, the women's movement began to pick up steam. Unequal pay in the workforce sparked the national women's movement of the 1960s and 1970s. In

---

[1] The old way of determining the divorce rate was to calculate the percentage of marriages ending in divorce (i.e., in 1979 the divorce rate was 50%). This approach was changed to reflect a more accurate way of account for divorces. The new divorce rate is identified by the number of divorces per 1,000 married women age 15 and older (National Marriage Project and the Institute for American Values, 2012).
[2] Cherlin, A (1992)

1963, women were only making 59% of what men were making[3]. This era of independence gave women the confidence to know that they could both work and take care of their children.

There is no shortage of reasons why the divorce rate climbed so high in the United States and remains there to this day: lack of communication skills, finances, infidelity, loss of interest, (including sexual desire), abuse, and the list goes on and on. It could be one reason or multiple reasons. It could be his fault, her fault, or their fault. I'm not trying to assign blame here.

Because there are so many reasons why couples get divorced, I don't think our "problems" are the problem. There has never been a shortage of problems a married couple will experience. There never will be. But the facts are clear: somewhere between 40% and 50% of marriages fail for one reason or another.[4]

Why is that? Is something wrong with the institution of marriage itself? A growing number of couples have opted to live together without getting married. Are they better off

---

[3] http://www.infoplease.com/spot/equalpayact1.html
[4] National Marriage Project and the Institute for American Values, 2012

than the married couple? Nope! The mortality rate of their relationships is just as high, if not higher than the married couples.

From a Christian perspective, cohabitation is shunned and divorce is discouraged. But I'm not naïve. I know both are realities for some Christians. So what's the formula for a Christian who wants to eventually marry and live happily ever after?

The Cultural Shift

In the United States, we have witnessed a shift from what Warner, Lee, & Lee called a patriarchal society, where marriages were uniformly husband-dominated.[5] Over the last several decades we have experienced a shift to a more egalitarian society, where marital resources and decision-making are managed equally.

Women are more independent. Gone are the days when a woman lived with her parents until she got married. The most recent research suggests that is because people are waiting longer to marry. The median age at first marriage

---

[5] Warner, Lee, & Lee (1986)

went from 20.3 for women and 22.8 for men in 1960 to 26.5 and 28.7, respectively, in 2011[6]

Nowadays, a woman has her own apartment or house, her own car, and her own career. In some cities she might make more money than her male contemporaries. She is self-sufficient and doesn't rely on a man for financial means. So it's not going to be easy for her to hand over all that autonomy to a man she feels doesn't show good judgment or make good decisions. For some women, that's a no-go from the start. Women who find themselves in such relationships are choosing to get out of them.

Many women in the current generation were raised by their mothers and taught not to depend on a man. They have proven that they can stand on their own two feet and raise the family by themselves. They've seen their mother do it. They have friends and family members who did it. Keeping a man is an option of convenience. If his judgment and decision-making doesn't diminish the quality of life she's able to achieve on her own, then she'll keep him. If his decisions show a lack of judgment and begin to negatively impact her, then he's expendable.

---

[6] National Marriage Project and the Institute for American Values, 2012

In this book, I will introduce you to a leadership model that is designed specifically for couples, whether they are married, engaged, or in a committed dating relationship. This go-to guide is primarily intended to teach men how to be a leader in these relationships...whether they know how to lead, were never taught, or were taught leadership skills within a different context like the military, sports, or business. This is a simple, easy-to-follow crash course on how to be the man your mate trusts, respects, and actually wants to follow.

The instructions herein will teach you the simple four-step process to provide leadership in your relationship. It will teach you how to think as a leader. You will learn how to:

1. Become an expert decision-maker by learning how and when to use intuition to make sound judgments and wise, accurate decisions quickly.

2. Use power to gain influence in your relationship.

3. Determine what to say as a leader, when to say it, and how to say it to persuade your mate to follow a specific course of action.

4. Identify what information to consider in making decisions and what data to overlook.

5. Identify solutions before the problems arrive.

A Christian Perspective on Relationships

From a Christian perspective, biblical tenets stipulate a wife is supposed to submit to her husband. This is scary for many women. It's not that they're scared to submit. If fact, most Christian woman I've met really want to submit to their current or future husband. They're scared to submit to a man *they don't trust*. And if she doesn't trust him, she definitely is considering leaving. And that's what's currently happening on a large scale, inside the Christian community and out.

I'm not saying that it's the husband's fault relationships end. Women share the blame in break-ups. But I am saying Christian women are looking for a man who has good judgment. If he can't do a better job managing their life than she can, or if she becomes disgruntled with her husband's decision-making in leading the family, she's no longer financially dependent on him to stay like she would have been before World War II.

The man is responsible for leading the family. Now...I'm not saying that women aren't leaders or can't provide leadership too. Women are empowered and capable leaders. In working with couples in my relationship consulting business, The Family Bootcamp™, what I'm seeing now is a lapse in leadership by men who have an opportunity to take on a leadership role in their family, but are readily willing to step back and let her lead everything. This is the very issue that got Adam in trouble and brought sin into the world. When Adam should have taken the lead and prevented Eve from eating fruit from the forbidden tree, he stepped back and let Eve make the decision to eat the fruit.

Why are men so willing to step back now? Maybe they were never taught to lead, they don't know how to lead, or they are unprepared for the magnitude of the responsibility that leadership requires. Regardless of the reason, this absence of leadership affects their children and society as a whole. One out of four children will grow up in a home without a father and this absence leaves a huge hole.[7] We are seeing the aftermath in the news every day. A 1992

---

[7] U.S. Census Bureau. America's Families and Living Arrangements: 2011. Table C9. Children by Presence and Type of Parent(s), Race, and Hispanic Origin. Washington, DC: U.S. Census Bureau.

study reported that 85 percent of all youth in prisons grew up in a fatherless home. Twenty years later, these young boys that grew up without their fathers have children of their own, who are also growing up without their father. It's a horrible cycle that needs to be addressed on a national scale.

If you were a child in the 70s and 80s when the divorce rate was approaching 50%, there's a good chance you grew up in a single-parent home. My parents fell within that curve.

After 17 years of marriage, my parents separated in 1983 when I was 13 years old. Fortunately for me, my dad moved 20 minutes away and remained very active in my life. He picked me up from football practice. He came to all my games. I could hear him in the stands over the entire crowd yelling my name when I ran an 80-yard touchdown. My sister and I stayed over his house every two weeks. Although my parents didn't live together, I had a father and mother who raised me. However, the sad reality is a lot of you weren't so fortunate. Once your dad left, he was gone. Or he was in and out of your life. You couldn't rely on him to be where he said he was going to be or do what he said he was going to do. Actually, the inverse is true: you could rely on him *not* being where he said he would be and *not* doing what he said he would do.

Leadership in Relationship

I tell couples all the time: the information you studied in sixth grade only prepared you to graduate from the sixth grade. You now have to learn seventh grade information to graduate from the seventh grade. Similarly in relationships, what you had to do to get her…you have to build upon that to keep her. That's what I had to do.

I realized that I was incapable of making my marriage work with the limited knowledge and leadership skills that I possessed when I got married. So I read, studied, got mentored, and even went back to college to learn how to be a better leader, eventually getting my master's degree in organizational leadership. And what I learned has helped me build upon the little bit of leadership skills I had by teaching me how to pursue our family goals while making sure my wife's input and interests were well represented. And that's what I'm going to share with you — a 4-step guide to provide leadership in your relationship.

However, this book is unlike anything you've ever read before from a Christian standpoint. To gain the clearest understanding of how to lead your family, I had to farm through the biblical text for the right theology that applies to God's function and design for the family. But I also had to comb through the outer perimeter of scholastic research, grafting in theories and principles from psychology, organizational leadership theory, neurological science, and marriage and family therapy principles. Combined, I have captured the full essence of how leadership functions within a relationship.

By the end of this book, you will know exactly what to do to lead your family. So let's start with a good, clear understanding of leadership...so you'll know when you can provide leadership and when you can't.

Part 1:
What Leadership Looks
Like in Relationships

God-Given Providence

I had absolutely no idea that I would venture down the path of devoting my life to enhancing the quality and stability of relationships. As a young boy I told myself, "When I grow up I want to be a football player, police officer, and a CIA and FBI super-secret agent." Then, in eighth grade, I saw my mother, who was a seamstress and public school teacher, take a raw piece of material and make an entire outfit from scratch in 30 minutes. I was astounded! I said to myself, "If I can learn how to sew, I can make a fresh new outfit every day before school! I could be the flyest dude in high school!" So from that point on, I wanted to be a famous fashion designer, like Giorgio Armani.

Following my passion, my mom taught me how to design clothes and sew. By high school, I still had dreams of being a fashion designer, but I didn't quite have the skills yet. So I concocted a fallback career after seeing the movie *Wall Street* in 1987. I was going to be a real estate mogul/stock investment tycoon like Gordon Gekko. "Yes, greed is good," I thought to myself. I also was going to go into business with my best friend and own a super cool jazz supper club/restaurant like Blues Alley in Washington, D.C.

In college, I majored in business management. A friend and I did a fashion show on campus, highlighting our designs. I was on my way! Four years later, with a new bachelor's degree, I didn't even apply for any jobs. I went out and launched my fashion empire in June. By August, I was retired. I was done! I realized I didn't like being cooped up in my room sewing all day. So what's next?

I got a temping job as a data entry clerk in the Maryland suburbs of Washington, D.C. But my entrepreneurial spirit was still alive, so I ventured into my fallback real estate mogul career with one of those "no-money down" real estate deals that used to come on TV at 2 a.m. That's the perfect Gordon Gekko-ish job for me! Right? Wrong. No haps! It never even got off the ground. What's next? Ah, the jazz supper club. But once I found out all the legal and financial requirements to open and maintain a restaurant that was a non-starter. What's next?

I attempted opening an arcade. Fail! I tried a network marketing company that sold water filtration units. Fail! I connected with a gentleman whose family won a contract to provide technology services to financial companies. Fraud-fail! He was a joke. I even tried resurrecting my fashion empire. Fail...again! By the age of 23, I had attempted and failed at every dream I had growing up. Trying to stay optimistic, I said to myself, "I found yet another career that I wasn't going to do. That just means I'm getting closer to discovering the one I'm going to be really good at."

Chapter 1:
The Marriage Organization

The Lunch Crew

It's Tuesday around noon. Several colleagues and I usually eat lunch together at work. We eat, drink, talk, laugh, joke, and get caught up on the latest events and drama in our respective lives. We randomly trickle in around the same time. We generally sit in the same area of the cafeteria. There are anywhere from three to six of us that meet on any given day. Today, I was the first one there. But I wasn't always first. In fact, I was the last one to be accepted into the group.

Before I ate with them, I would pass by them as I was leaving the cafeteria with my food on my way to eat at my desk. Occasionally I would stop and chat for two or three minutes. Those two or three turned into five, which turned into twenty.

Depending on how dramatic someone's story was or the comedic value of the rolling commentary from the group, I found myself standing by the table engulfed in their stories while my lunch was steady getting colder and colder. Finally they just invited me to sit down and eat my lunch instead of letting it get cold. That set the precedent. Over time, they accepted me as a regular member of the group.

The Group

You likely have some groups you're part of too. Maybe you have a similar lunch group or a group of guys you meet-up with to play basketball, golf, or poker. How and when did you first start meeting together? And what makes your group a group? These questions may seem meaningless at first. But it's actually critical to the success or failure of your relationship.

Understanding what makes up a group is important to your relationship with your mate or your future significant other. The makeup and structure of a group determines how members of the group interact with each other.

Ralph Stogdill, an Ohio State University professor, organizational theorist, and leadership research pioneer, was a brilliant man in his field. His vast body of research and academic accolades span more than 30 years, beginning in the 1940s. He was a student of people—more so, people within relationships. In his article, "Leadership, Membership, and Organization," he identified the most accurate definition of a group:[8]

> "A group is defined by two factors: 1) two or more people that perceive there is unity among them, and 2) those people are acting in a unified way toward society."

Based on Stogdill's definition, my lunch group meets the requirement for a group. We have perceived unity among us by regularly meeting for lunch together, and we act in a unified manner by talking, eating, laughing at the table together.

Groups versus Organizations

The terms *group* and *organization* are sometimes used interchangeably, yet they are structured differently. However, an organization is different than a group. Stogdill's explanation of an organization includes the dynamics of a group, in that there must be two or more people that perceive they are unified and they interact in a unified manner. But further research found that the makeup

---

[8] Stogdill, 1950

and structure of these groups involve them achieving a common goal or purpose.[9] And the persons within these groups have different responsibilities, or roles, that lead toward accomplishing these common goals or purposes.

Citing sociologist Florian Znaniecki's research, Stogdill asserts:

"...some of them act as organizers, leaders, or coordinators of the regular activities of others with reference to the common purpose...Not all of these individuals need be continuously active; indeed, in many groups a considerable proportion remain passive, acting only in reaction to the actions of others."

So in Stogdill's view, the difference between a group and an organization is an organization has a common goal or purpose and a group does not; and the members of the organization have different roles and responsibilities that lead towards accomplishing those goals.

What does this have to do with your relationship...and the interaction therein? Some of you interact with your mate like you're in a group. You have no common goals or

---

[9] Znaniecki, 1945

purpose; you have no defined roles. You both do whatever *you* think is right. While others of you interact with each other like you're in an organization. You have common family goals, roles, and responsibilities. And get this—in some relationships, one person may interact like they're in a group, while the other acts like they're in an organization.

To explain this phenomenon, we have to go all the way back to the first chapter in the first book of the Bible.

Genesis 1

Most people are familiar with what happens in the first chapter of Genesis, but for the sake of those who don't know, here's a very brief overview: God created the heavens and the earth. Over a period of five days He proceeds to go through a series of "Let there be's" and created everything. And after every "Let there be...," he said what he created was good.

Up to this point, God had not created man yet. Verses 26 and 27 established God's intent: "*26 Then God said, "Let us make man in our image, after our likeness..."* By "man" He was referring to the generic term for mankind. "*27 So*

God created man in his own image, in the image of God he created him; male and female he created them." "

Here's where it gets interesting: In Genesis 1:28, God gives mankind, both male and female, three tasks. *"And God blessed them. And God said to them, "1) Be fruitful and multiply and fill the earth and 2) subdue it and 3) have dominion over* [to rule] *the fish of the sea and over the birds of the heavens and over every living thing that moves on the earth."*

Take special note that in the first chapter of Genesis, God created everything that mankind would need to survive and accomplish the three goals even before He created them. It wasn't until Genesis 2:7 that God continued to paint the rest of the picture. God breathed life into the male and he became a living being. Immediately, God created a garden and put him in it to do what he created him to do: *"work it and take care of it"* (Genesis 2:15). In so doing, male began subduing the vegetation of the land.

To rule the land, God *"…brought [the animals] to the man to see what he would name them; and whatever the man called each living creature, that was its name."* But there was no way for him to accomplish the first task—fill the earth—by himself. So God said, "*It is not good for man to be alone. I will make a helper suitable for him*" (Genesis 2:18).

So God caused a deep sleep to fall upon the man. He took one of his ribs, closed up its place with flesh, and made it into a woman. Then he presented her to the man. (Genesis 2:20-22).

The First Family

Now we have the first family ever created: Adam the husband and Eve the wife. The three goals assigned to them did not change once they became a family. They were still responsible for filling, subduing, and ruling over the earth.

But how would they do it? They did it by carrying out the roles and responsibilities they were assigned. As outlined in Genesis 2:15-22, together they would fill the earth. To subdue and rule the land, the man's role was to "work the land and take care of it." The female's role was to be the suitable "*helper*."

Is Marriage an Organization?

What does all this have to do with your marriage or relationship? I submit to you this...marriage does not function as a group. The institution of marriage, the way God originally created it, operates as an organization.

Let's compare the two according to Stogdill's definition of an organization:

Organizations	*Marriages*
Organizations consist of a group of two or more people	Marriages consist of a group of two people
Organizations must have a common purpose or goal	Marriages have a common purpose or goal to fill, subdue, and rule
Organizations contain members that have certain roles and responsibilities that lead towards accomplishing the common purpose or goal	In marriages, the male's role and responsibility is "to work it and take care of it," while the female's role is to be a "suitable helper"

Table 1. Marriage versus Organization Comparison

According to scripture, God created marriage as a model of his relationship between Christ and the church (Ephesians 5:32). In so doing, the model He created has the exact same structure, form, and function of an organization.

God-Given Instruction

Now that all of my life's plans were dashed, I was broke from failed business endeavors and emotionally dejected. I realized that my plans for my life weren't working. So I figured I would not plan my next move—I would give God a shot at it, since I had recently been introduced to the church. This was a big step for me because I had been actively planning my career since I was 13. Now at 23, I was about to relinquish control of my own life and turn it over to the unknown.

To my surprise, God's plan for my life was for me to do nothing for the next seven years. At least that's what it felt like to me. Actually, His plan was for me was to sit down, shut up, listen, and learn.

Learn what? Learn about being a man, learn about women, learn how to get rid of my young foolish ways, learn about relationships, learn about love, learn about marriage, and learn about family. Through the tutelage of the pastor of my church and his wife, I learned about the purposes of men, women, love, marriage, and the family. Most importantly, I learned how God's love served as a model for how a husband and wife should demonstrate their love for each other. His example was given to us so that we could see why and how to carry out His master plan for our families, and then raise our children to do the same.

Chapter 2:
Let's Talk About Leadership

Leadership Versus Leadership

The concept of leadership is a relatively new field of study compared to other social sciences such as psychology, sociology, and anthropology, which have been studied for centuries. Leadership as a legitimate discipline of study has only been around since the 1920s. But throughout its nine decades of research, psychologists, scholars, and academics appeared to be competing against each other to try to define what leadership is.

The first group of psychologists who took a stab at defining leadership in the 1930s looked at great leaders, like Julius Caesar, Napoleon, and Winston Churchill. They concluded that certain persons were *born* with a set of personality traits that made them great leaders. That was called the Great Person Theory.

Then the next set of researchers came along in the '40s and debunked that theory. Their findings supported what was known as the Personal Traits Theory of Leadership.

This theory identified personal traits and attributes highly effective leaders possessed. This was a departure from the Great Person Theory in that it said you could acquire these personal traits through experience and become a great leader. You didn't have to be born with them.

About every decade thereafter, another set of researchers came along to debunk the previous theory and replace it with their more up-to-date concept.

I'm not going to repeat this same pattern—trying to coin a new definition or style of leadership just because I'm writing a book about men, marriage, and leadership. Instead, I set out to identify what all researchers agreed upon. In looking through the 90+ years of leadership research, I found four central themes that ran through all the definitions.

Leadership: The Four Themes that Define It

Through the decades, researchers have used different terminology to explain their research and justify their theories of what leadership is and isn't. Even though the previous decades' theories were debunked, four specific themes kept resurfacing each decade:

Themes	Descriptions
Process	Multiple steps, defined or undefined, or a series of steps or actions, as opposed to a single step or action
Influence	The act of controlling, persuading, causing an entity to move, respond, act, or not act in a certain way
People	A group of two or more people
Purpose	A specific direction, result, defined goal, or outcome

Out of the hundreds of different definitions for leadership, I found Ralph Stogdill's definition of leadership captured these four themes in one simple definition:

Leadership is the process of influencing the movement of a group toward a particular outcome (Stogdill, 1950).

Therefore, it will serve as our working definition for what we will hereafter refer to as leadership.

How Leadership Works Inside an Organization

In your job, you likely have a group of coworkers who perform different duties than you. And your office also has a set of goals that you and your coworkers were hired to accomplish. Your job is therefore considered an organization.

Not only is your job an organization, but so is your fraternity or sorority, church, children's PTA, motorcycle club, etc. And yes…your marriage is an organization too.

This brings me to the first rule of leadership: Leadership *only* exists inside an organization. There must be a group and a common goal it's moving toward in order for someone to lead the group in that direction. Conversely, leadership cannot exist inside a group because it doesn't have a common goal. Even if you're in a group with a common goal, if everybody's doing the same thing, there's no difference in the roles or responsibilities. No one is taking on the responsibility of organizing or coordinating the activities in an effort to accomplish the common goal, as Znaniecki described. So no leadership exists.

All three components must be present in order for leadership to exist:
1. A group,
2. A common goal, and
3. Different roles and responsibilities

It's like a group of men paddling in a canoe down a river. If everybody is just paddling as he sees fit, no leadership exists. Somebody needs to take the responsibility of charting the course, setting the cadence, giving instructions on which sides each man should row, etc.

There was no leadership in my lunch group. We all just showed up with lunch in hand, ate, and went our separate ways. If someone didn't eat lunch on a particular day, it was no big deal. No one called him to motivate him to rejoin our group. He just wasn't there. There was no process established to influence anyone to show up at lunch, even though our group had a common goal of eating lunch together. We all performed the same task—we ate our own lunch. Thus, there was no leadership.

Leadership Lessons In High School Football

In high school, I played football at John F. Kennedy High School in Silver Spring, Maryland (go Cavaliers!). I played running back and cornerback my sophomore and senior years. (I also was the kickoff returner and returned one 80 yards to the house for a touchdown. This has nothing to do with leadership; I just wanted to flex nostalgically. OK, back to my analogy.)

Let's look at the three criteria for an organization and see if my football team qualifies.

- One, there was a group of 60+ young men who bonded together as teammates. *Check.*

- Two, there was a defined goal for the team—win football games. *Check.*

- Three, there were different people playing different positions that led toward accomplishing our goal. *Check.*

My high school football team was an organization. And where there is an organization, there must be leadership present, right? Coach Ripatoe was the leader of the offensive. Coach Lieberman was the defensive-backs coach. And the one who provided leadership to the whole football team was our head coach, Coach Straub.

Travel about 15 minutes west on the same road and you'll reach our school's arch rival, Wheaton High School. For decades, Kennedy and Wheaton couldn't stand each other, partially because our schools were on the same street. But also because some of the students who went to elementary and junior high school together moved into Wheaton's school district and went there for high school.

We played them twice every year. I especially wanted to crush Wheaton because of Bill, a childhood friend from my neighborhood. We competed at everything! Dodgeball, tag, hide-n-seek, kickball, jump rope, swimming, foot races, you name it. We even competed to see who could spit the furthest.

So when he moved to a new neighborhood and started playing football at Wheaton, it was my duty...no, my *obligation* to show him my reign of dominance extended beyond our neighborhood and onto the football field. As the running back, instead of avoiding Bill, who played defensive safety, I'd try to find him and bulldoze right through him.

In spite of our contempt for Wheaton's football team, they had the exact same organizational structure as

Kennedy's football team; and they too were considered an organization. The head coach on Wheaton's team was also the main person who influenced the team to win their games. He probably made his team run sprints, tackling drills, and hold those doggone two-a-day practices in the July and August heat like Coach Straub did. Both of these coaches were providing leadership.

Now what if Wheaton's head coach came over to our practice and started coaching us, telling us to run sprints, do circuits, and calling plays for our offense? "Officer, see, what-had-happened-was, Wheaton's head coach came into our practice and then...yada...yada...yada. And that's when the fight started."

Or what if during our game against Wheaton, their coach started barking out defensive coverages to our secondary, and telling the linebackers when and where to blitz. "Officer, see, what-had-happened-was, Wheaton's head coach started calling plays for our defense...yada...yada...yada. And that's when the bench-clearing brawl started."

The notion that a head coach from another team would attempt to provide leadership to an opposing team is ludicrous. The reason why it's so absurd is because leadership only exists *inside* of an organization.

Can the president of Russia contact the U.S. Department of Defense and instruct them on military strategy? No, that's called sabotage, not leadership. Can a pastor from another church walk into your church and start telling the staff and congregants how things will be run? Heavens no!

If you're not a part of the organization, then you cannot provide leadership, even if you are recognized as the one who provides leadership in their own organization. Once you step outside the boundaries of your own organization, your leadership is nullified.

This is the reason why a man can't stand their woman talking to someone else about what goes on within their relationship—especially if it's another man. To him, those dudes are not a part of their group.

Leadership & Leaders

Up until now, I have avoided using the term "leader." I did so intentionally because throughout the breadth of leadership research, the words leader and leadership are often used interchangeably. This causes confusion when trying to accurately explain what leadership is.

My former supervisor in the Office of Human Resources, at my first "real" job after college, was a great leader. She was friendly, easy to talk to, and created a fun and comfortable work environment; but she was no-nonsense when it came to getting your work done correctly and on time. Every supervisor I've had since was measured by her standard of leadership.

When a qualifier is used to describe what kind of leader a person is—"she's a great leader"—that description does not define what a leader is. A leader simply is the one who provides leadership —good, bad, or otherwise.

5 Things Leadership is NOT

1. A leader is not character specific.

There can actually be a supervisor that is a good leader and another supervisor that's a bad leader. As long as they both are the ones providing leadership in their organizations, they both are considered leaders. That's because leadership is not character specific. 'Good' and 'bad' only describe the quality of leadership they provide.

2. Leadership is not person specific.

The existence of an organization and the leadership therein does not dictate who the leader is. Anyone in an organization can be the leader, not just the person(s) in a position of authority. For, leadership is not authority.

Stogdill defines authority as the permissions given to someone to make decisions, carry out responsibilities, and enlist the cooperation of others.[10] But just because you have the authority to provide leadership doesn't mean you're the one providing leadership, or in fact, that you even know *how* to provide leadership.

This misunderstanding between authority and leadership is what sometimes stumps men in relationships. I've seen countless husbands who find themselves in a power struggle with their mate over who will get their way. They try to assert their authority to gain the upper hand. "I'm the man of the house!" is their war cry. And yes you are, good sir, the man of the house. And if you're a Christian, by default that means you are assigned the role and responsibility as the head of your organizational family.

---

[10] Stogdill, 1950

But that's just a position of authority. It doesn't mean you actually *are* the leader, nor does it mean that you know what to do to provide leadership. That's because leadership is not person-specific.

For example, in the unwritten rules of pick-up basketball, it's universally known that, "I got next!" means that *I* have the authority to pick up any four players *I* choose to run on *my* squad. Everybody knows it. Even if somebody comes to the court later, they will first check to see who has the authority to play the next game by asking, "Who's got next?"

"I do," I'll say confidently.

"You got your five?"

"Yeah."

Then they will say, "I got next after you." Done deal. No discussion...no issue. And at the end of the current game, *I'm* going on the court with *my* four players to play the winners.

When the game begins, everybody plays their role and performs the responsibilities assigned to it. As we play,

41

there usually arises someone on my team who is superiorly skilled (suffice it to say, it's usually not me). He has a command of the court and a hot hand. He's the one telling people on *my* team what to do, who to pick up, running the fast breaks, stealing the ball, etc.

Eventually, everyone on *my* team is playing up to his energy level, following his instructions, and passing him the ball as the go-to guy. And if we win, the elation is felt throughout *my* whole team, but our success is primarily due to his efforts. Now you tell me: who had the authority and who provided leadership to *my* team?

3. Leadership is not direction specific.

Remember, leadership is the process of influencing the movement of a group toward a particular outcome. Look at the executive leaders at Enron, for example. They led that company right into bankruptcy and ultimately out of business. Or look at Ponzi scheme architect Bernie Madoff. Through lies and deceit, he led hundreds of investors in a financial house of cards that came toppling down. Some investors lost all their money. Some even lost their entire retirement savings.

This just goes to show you that leadership is not direction specific. It doesn't matter in what direction a person is leading you, whoever is influencing the group in one direction or another, that person is providing leadership.

4. Leadership is not outcome specific.

My basketball team definitely had leadership. But what if we lost? Was there still leadership present? Of course! For, leadership is not outcome-specific. Losing the game does not negate the fact that leadership was present and that Mr. Hot Hands was the leader providing it.

5. Leadership is not purpose specific.

I used this basketball example to explain what leadership is *not*. But it's clearly obvious that leadership is not limited to just basketball or a high school football team. It does not matter whether it is a game of pickup basketball, a reality show dance team, a singing group, street gang, your marriage, or your relationship with your fiancée, leadership is not purpose specific. As long as the three essential elements of an organization exist, leadership is always present.

Biblical Examples of Leaders and Leadership

If the argument is true that leadership is the *process of influencing the movement of a group toward a particular direction or outcome,* and the one who is providing leadership is the leader, then this structure of leadership should be true in biblical relationships that are structured like an organization. So let's look at some and see if these two definitions hold true.

Let me repeat my caveat. I'm not suggesting that biblical relationships were designed to be organizations. God did not say, "Let there be relationships in the likeness of an organization." I am saying, however, that wherever biblical relationships are structured like an organization, leadership exists.

We are going to look at both examples from both the Old and New Testament, with Moses, John the Baptist, Noah, and Paul.

Moses

Moses did a lot with his days on earth, but I am just going to focus on when Moses led the Israelites out of Egypt (Exodus 3:1–4:31). God started off Moses' journey with the command, "*Come, I will send you to Pharaoh that you may bring my people, the children of Israel, out of Egypt*" (Exodus 3:10). That was his goal.

Moses was initially reluctant to do it because he was "slow of speech and tongue." So God appointed his brother Aaron to be his spokesman. God would speak to Moses and tell him what to do. Moses would tell Aaron. And Aaron would tell the people. Since there were at least two people, a goal, and different roles and responsibilities toward accomplishing that goal, they were officially considered an organization. But soon there would be more people added to their group.

Moses and Aaron had a meeting with all the elders of Israel to convince them to join their cause. Now their organization had more members and more roles and responsibilities. Moses was the leader who received God's instructions, Aaron was the spokesman for Moses, and the elders would communicate the message to all the people of Israel.

With that information alone, we can conclude that Moses was a leader and did provide leadership to the Israelite people.

John the Baptist

The stories about John the Baptist are accounted in all four books of the Gospel (Matthew 3, Mark 1, Luke 1 & 3, and John 1 & 3]. However, we'll look at the book of Luke because it gives the most detail about his life and mission.

John's father, Zechariah, was a priest in the temple. And his mother, Elizabeth, was barren. One day when Zack was burning incense in the temple, an angel came to him and Liz (yes...I gave them nicknames). The angel said Zack was going to have a son and he was to be named John. "*And he will turn many of the children of Israel to the Lord their God, and he will go before him in the spirit and power of Elijah, to turn the hearts of the fathers to the children, and the disobedient to the wisdom of the just, to make ready for the Lord a people prepared*" (Luke 1:18).

That was John's purpose.

The groups of people included within this purpose were the 1) "many children of Israel," 2) "him"—the angel was speaking about Jesus, 3) "fathers," 4) "the disobedient," and 5) "the Lord." This represented a diverse population with a variety of different interests. But by definition, this large coalition of individuals and segmented groups of society was still considered an organization because they all had a common goal…"turning to the Lord their God." And they all had different roles and responsibilities toward that end.

When John was older, he was preaching and calling these groups to repent (Matthew 3:1-2) and baptizing these groups in the Jordan River (Matthew 3:6). These were his responsibilities linked to the purpose assigned to him before he was born. Therefore, John the Baptist must be considered a leader.

Noah

Noah's claim to fame was his obedience to God when he was commanded to build an ark in Genesis 6:9-8-19. God was fed up with how corrupt and violent the world had become. So he decided to destroy it. He gave Noah specific dimensions and instructions for how to build an ark. So Noah built the ark as instructed.

God told Noah to take his wife, his three sons, their wives and children, food, every animal and bird, and enter the ark. Then God unleashed 40 days and nights of rain. They stayed in the ark for nearly 12 months until God told them to leave the arc.

Did Noah provide leadership? Let's see. Was there a specific goal? Yes, to build an ark. Contrary to the movie *Noah*, scripture does not indicate that anyone helped him build it, not even his sons. It looks like he built it by himself. There was no group for Noah to influence toward the goal of building the ark. Since there was no group, there was no organization in which to provide leadership. Therefore, Noah did not provide leadership in building the ark.

The Apostle Paul

Paul's biblical exploits are so numerous that we'll just look at one instance where Paul had an opportunity to lead.

First, a little backstory: before Paul was converted, his name was Saul. And Saul, by order of the Chief Priest, led a roving band of thugs to Damascus to kidnap and kill any post-resurrection followers of Jesus found belonging to "The Way" (Acts 9:1-2). That meets the leadership criteria in and of itself for Saul. But that was before Saul's conversion to Paul.

Paul's purpose was made known to him on his trip of rendition to Damascus (Acts 9:3-22). The Lord blinded Saul's vision. The men he was leading took him to Judas' house in Damascus where he stayed for three days. While Saul was at Judas' house, God payed a visit to a man named Ananias. He told Ananias to go to Judas' house and lay hands on Saul so he would regain his sight because *"...he is a chosen instrument of mine to carry my name before the Gentiles and kings and the children of Israel. For I will show him how much he must suffer for the sake of my name."* (Acts 9:15-16).

This was Paul's purpose.

Sometime later, Barnabas, a fellow follower, went to get Saul from his hometown, Tarsus, to teach the Gentiles and Jews at the church in Antioch (Acts 11:25-26). This was the first time Paul began to fulfill his purpose and become a leader as a Christian. The Antioch church made up the group. Teaching the Gentiles and Jews about the gospel of Jesus Christ was their common goal. And Paul was assigned the role of teacher to lead them to that end.

There are hundreds of other examples of biblical leadership that exist in the Bible. Leadership, in and of itself, is neither biblical nor secular, right nor wrong, good nor bad. Scholars, practitioners, ministers, and politicians alike have wrongly used these descriptors to define what leadership is, or whether someone is a leader based on the outcome. But these adjectives are merely describing the quality of leadership provided in the organization.

So, regardless how good or bad the leadership is, who's providing it, the purpose, direction, or the outcome, leadership only exists inside an organization. And the person providing it is the leader.

God-Given Process

1993 started a new chapter in my life. I turned 23 and landed a permanent job with the federal government. I closed on a house and bought a new SUV the same weekend. It was a small two-bedroom single family home, but it was mine! And my mortgage was only $519 a month. Ah, those were the days! During my early 20s, I partook in the classic youthful tomfoolery and hijinks that young men often do. But I knew that if the woman of my dreams came along, I would do something to ruin the relationship and miss out on the woman of a lifetime. So I embarked on a quest to purge my tomfoolery ways and abandon the hijinks that I'd grown fond of.

So in the summer of 1994, when I was 24 years old, I decided I wanted to be married by 27. I figured I would likely be purged of my tomfoolery and hijinks by then. I also wanted my wedding in the fall because that is my favorite season and I wanted us to go on future anniversary trips in the fall when the leaves were changing and it isn't too cold. So the wedding would be in October 1997.

I also wanted to be engaged for a year. I figured I only needed a month to convince someone to marry me. So I had to pick my fiancée by September 1996 and convince her to marry me by October 1996 to meet my year-long engagement period

At that time, I wasn't dating anyone and hadn't had a girlfriend since high school. I mounted what turned out to be a two-year process of observation, assessment, and evaluation to find the right woman. I curated a mental list of qualities I knew that I wanted in a wife...and character flaws I knew I didn't want. Whoever met the criteria made the list. Conversely, no matter how fine she was, the extent of our previous relationship, or how much I liked her, if she didn't meet the criteria, she didn't make the list.

During those two years, I began to mature. I gradually cut back friends who were a part of that old life. I eventually stopped going to my old stomping grounds. I got more serious about my relationship with the Lord. Basically, I just started to grow up.

All my friends who knew about this plan thought I was crazy. They all wondered how I could marry some random chick I had not been dating. And how I thought some random chick would want to marry me having never dated me. Truthfully, I didn't have the answer. I just knew if I found the right one, there wasn't anything I would not do to get her. And 30 days was all I needed

One of my co-workers, BerNadette, also thought my plan was crazy. We worked on the same team. We shared a lot of our personal lives, stories, etc. I knew all about her issues and past relationships and she knew about mine. We built a close friendship. So close, that I looked up one day and discovered that, although we were complete opposites, she met the criteria. This was a surprise to me because she had always just been Bernie, my co-worker. So I had to keep a close eye on her because my list was down to three and my September 1996 deadline was drawing near.

Chapter 3:
Leadership in Marriage

Organizationally Structured Relationships

Some time ago, I hosted a small men's group meeting at our house. About six men showed up. One of the guys, who we'll call Trey, was lamenting about how he and his wife, who we'll call, Paula, had been struggling for last nine years of their twelve-year marriage. The D-word had been floated several times. Both being Christians, they wanted to try to make it work but didn't really know what else to do to turn the tide. They tried marriage counseling, marriage conferences, and even accountability partners. But none of them seemed to work.

After some probing, I gained a sense of what the main issues were. One of the issues was that their marriage was operating as a group rather than an organization. But remember, God didn't create marriage as a group, but as an organization with three common goals: to fill, subdue, and rule. And each person in the marriage has a role and responsibility: the male is "to work it and take care of it," while the female is to be a "suitable helper." But there was no common goal in their marriage...let alone different roles and responsibilities.

Trey and Paula have three children, so they got the "fill" goal taken care of. And they each had different roles to perform towards accomplishing that goal, which I think you can figure out. However, they didn't know what God wanted them to subdue or rule together as a family.

Since they didn't have these common goals to pursue, they didn't have defined roles or responsibilities in their relationship. Each person did whatever they felt necessary at the time according to their own understanding and individual preferences. Because these two critical pieces of their relationship were missing, there was no leadership in their marriage.

As a result, their individual decisions were causing major problems for the past nine years. They disagreed on everything from the finances, to family priorities, to the amount of time spent at work. Intimacy, sex, quality time— out of the question! Communication? Only when there were issues concerning the children or to coordinate their schedules.

Trey and Paula's marriage is a prime example of the lack of a proper organizational structure for a marriage. So, if you are married, engaged, or are preparing to take your relationship anywhere near those two arenas, you must structure your relationship as an organization if you don't want it to ultimately fail.

Marriage and Leadership versus Your Marriage and Leadership

In fairness to this couple, the need for an organizationally structured relationship is not common knowledge. This relational dynamic is not often covered in premarital classes or marriage seminars and workshops. They mostly talk about making a date night, learning good communication skills, and being willing to compromise. No harm in that...right? We'd agree those are necessary skills to learn. But those skills sets work best within the context of an organizationally structured relationship.

Applying those skills outside of this structure is like telling actors in a play to use good enunciation, have good timing, and proper stage-blocking techniques when acting in a poorly written play. It doesn't matter if the entire play was cast with Tony Award-winning actors; it would still be a horrible play.

It's the same with a relationship that is not structured properly. You might be communicating, "I want to buy an RV and travel with the family on the weekends." And she's communicating, "I want to max out my retirement contribution so we can live comfortably during our retirement in 25 years." Both are noble pursuits. But there's no common goal the two of you are trying to accomplish. So regardless how great you both communicate, you're operating as a group and not an organization. There will forever be a disconnect.

Even if you end up going on a date night, you'll get into an argument at dinner over how much money to put down and what the monthly RV payment will be versus how much to increase her retirement contribution per pay period. There is no substitute for an organizational relationship. Without that, your relationship is a nothing more than a group of two people, with individual goals, who are great communicators, going on date nights.

But know this: if you ever want to have a relationship that's more than a self-indulging, self-gratifying experience of relational masturbation, then you must structure your relationship to operate as an organization. You must be in a relationship where there is a common goal and specific roles and responsibilities assigned to each person. There must be leadership that leads the relationship toward accomplishing its goals.

So knowing the common goal for your relationship is paramount. How can you provide leadership if you don't know what your duties are to fill, subdue, and rule? You don't! But what might happen though…is you end up miserable for the next nine out of 12 years in your marriage. And do you really want that?

Common Goals: Task-Oriented Goals versus Purpose-Oriented Goals

If you're married or engaged, does your relationship have common goals? I'm not talking about what are called task-oriented goals. Those are the goals that involve the rudimentary tasks of life, your typical honey-do list. "Honey, we have to paint the bedroom. Honey, we have to do this and that."

The common goals that were outlined in the first chapter of Genesis are purpose-oriented goals. These kinds of goals establish the direction or purpose for your family. They identify what behavior will and will not define the culture of your household. They establish how the children will be parented and what neighborhood your family will live in. They help you decide how the two of you will manage while one spouse goes back to school. They help you figure out how the two of you will assist your daughter, who is now a single parent. This magnitude of scale is what purpose-oriented goals are.

Equipped to Accomplish Your Purpose-Oriented Goal

It's extremely important for you to know your common goals—your purpose-oriented goals. God embedded in you the specific gifts and abilities needed to fill, subdue and rule the earth according to His plans for you. The Apostle Paul, in his letters to the churches in both Rome and Corinth, spoke about these unique gifts that God gave each person.

> "*Just as each of us has one body with many members, and these members do not all have the same function, so in Christ we who are many form*

one body, and each member belongs to all the others. We have different gifts, according to the grace given us..." (Romans 12:4-6)

This "grace" is a unique gift that God has given to those who are Christians.

"There are different kinds of gifts, but the same Spirit. There are different kinds of service, but the same Lord. There are different kinds of working, but the same God works all of them in all men. Now to each one the manifestation of the Spirit is given for the common good...All these are the work of one and the same Spirit, and he gives them to each one, just as he determines." (1 Corinthians 12:4-7; 11)

The unique purpose God created you for and the accompanying gifts He gave you with which to accomplish it are inextricably tied to the purpose-oriented goal that you are supposed to figure out and pursue. Now, to be true to the intent of these scriptures, they do not apply to any and everything you want to do. This is not a blank check for you to take your skills and abilities and do whatever you want with them "in the name of the Lawd." Nor do these passages give you license to take those God-given gifts and pimp them out for selfish indulgences. Nor can you claim for yourself gifts you want, or seen someone else have, that He did not give to you.

The context of these two passages is solely tied to those who are "in Christ." And you are supposed to use the "different gifts, according to the grace given" to you, the way God has already chosen to "work all of them" in you.

For the purposes of our discussion, the overall scope of this book is targeted toward purpose-oriented goals. However, mastering task-oriented goals is essential to learning how to pursue your purpose-oriented goals. In fact, those who have a difficult time navigating the task-oriented goals will have an even more difficult time grasping how to wade through the steep waters of executing purpose-oriented tasks, especially when you add the complexities of a spouse and/or children to your fleet. Handily grasping task-oriented goals will prove to be a huge asset in every future leadership endeavor hereafter.

Roles and Responsibilities within a Marriage

Function versus Design

If you are one of the fortunate ones to have a great understanding of relationships and have a purpose-oriented goal that you are pursuing, that's outstanding! But taking it another step further, does your relationship have specific roles and responsibilities related to your purpose-oriented goals?

God created everyone on purpose, for a purpose, and with a purpose. God didn't haphazardly throw everything together and say, "Whew! I'm tired of all this creating business. Everything looks good to me. I'm *done*! I'm going to get some rest." Not in the least! Roles and responsibilities are determined by the purpose of the individual and the purpose of the relationship.

I have several friends who are engineers. There's a phrase engineers use when they're designing a product: function before design. Before an engineer starts designing a product, he must first determine its function or purpose, for purpose determines how it will be designed.

Likewise, in creation, God first determined the function for a man and woman. Then he designed them accordingly. The woman's function is to carry a baby, so her body is designed with the necessary equipment to fulfill that function. The man's function is to impregnate the woman with a baby. So his body is designed to be a baby impregnating delivery system to fulfill that function.

Marital Roles and Responsibilities

Woven into the fabric of your mind, body, and soul are a unique set of skills, abilities, and gifts given to you by God (Exodus 31:1-6; Romans 12:6-8; 1 Corinthians 12:4-11). These unique skills, abilities, and gifts are the components He used to design you. Based on your unique design, he intends for you to carry out the specific purpose for which you were designed.

In general, marriage has a purpose too. And God designed it to have a man and a woman to carry out its purpose. Your roles and responsibilities in a marriage are first determined by your purpose, what God created you to do, and then by how He designed you to carry it out.

While each marriage is different, based on the skills, abilities, and gifts you have, the purpose of your marriage is directly tied to God's filling, subduing, and ruling agenda. That also means your specific roles and responsibilities within the marriage tie back to God's agenda. Every purpose-oriented common goal you have also ties back to God's agenda.

Priscilla and Aquila

Take the relationship of my favorite married couple in the Bible, Priscilla and Aquila. This couple opened up their home to Paul and showed him great hospitality by allowing him to stay with them for a year and a half while he worked as a tent-maker by day and preached in the synagogue at night.

When Paul left for the city of Ephesus, Priscilla and Aquila went with him. In Ephesus, they came across a young preacher named Apollos. He was thorough in the scripture, but only preached about the baptism of John and not about Jesus the Christ. Again, Priscilla and Aquila invited him into their new home in Ephesus to teach him about the scriptures more thoroughly. After they mentored him, Apollos vigorously debated the Jews in public to prove that Jesus was the Christ (Acts 18).

There are additional accounts recorded of Priscilla and Aquila showing hospitality. This wonderful couple inspires me, because even though scripture doesn't specifically state what their roles and responsibilities were, it's clear to me that their purpose was to show hospitality to preachers and evangelists as they passed through their town by welcoming them into their home, providing them support, teaching them when necessary, and allowing churches to meet in their home.

From all accounts, Priscilla and Aquila were doing their part to help subdue the earth by supporting the preachers who were spreading the Word of God. In my opinion, they are the perfect example of a couple who knows their roles and responsibilities and they faithfully performed them.

See why it is so important to know what your purpose-oriented goals are for your marriage? The entire scope and content of your marriage cascades down from that. If you don't know what your roles or responsibilities are, then take a look at the skills, abilities, and gifts God has given you. That's a clue in determining what they are.

Man's Roles versus Women's Roles

The way God designed you, with all your skills, abilities and gifts, is aligned with the roles He assigned for the man and woman in a marriage.

Remember, in the second chapter of Genesis, the man was assigned the responsibilities to "work and keep" the land; and the woman was to be a "suitable helper." These roles shouldn't conflict with each other. They should complement one another.

This design might be controversial and old-fashioned to some women who value women's economic and social freedom from a male-dominated society, or women who've experienced the effects of deadbeat/absentee/trifling men in their lives.

And know...I believe that this rise in women's freedom is the best thing that could happen for our society. This epidemic of deadbeat and absentee men is the cause of many of our socio-cultural problems in the country.

Regardless, the function and design of a marriage did not change. The Bible says, "Jesus Christ is the same yesterday, today, and forever" (Hebrews 13:8). God didn't change the structure when Adam deferred his leadership to Eve when she ate the fruit. He didn't change it when Jesus was born, and then killed by the very people He came to save. And He didn't change it when Holy Spirit came to take His place.

And now, even though women's experience with men is bleak, the structure of relationships still doesn't change. Husbands are still supposed to provide leadership and wives are still supposed to provide support and help. Let me be clear: do not confuse skills, abilities, and gifts with roles and responsibilities. I'm not saying that women aren't, can't, or shouldn't be leaders or provide leadership in their relationship. I'm not saying women should be seen but not heard. A woman might have better skills at planning and therefore is responsible for planning the family's activities. And her husband might have more creative skills and is responsible for helping his wife make the family activities more fun and exciting for the kids.

But whatever their respective skills, abilities, and gifts are, God has assigned the husband to be the one responsible for the family activities. So if something goes wrong, even if it is the woman's fault, God holds the man responsible. Because in God's eyes, the man is always responsible for everything that goes on in the family. No matter how skilled and gifted his wife is or how much she contributed to the activity, she is always his suitable helpmate, regardless of the current plight of her husband.

Just as a mother will always be the head of her son...regardless of how old he gets, so will a husband always be the head of his wife, regardless of how much he contributes to the family.

Know Your Role

So if you are not yet married, and you're in a committed relationship or engaged, know your role in an organizationally structured relationship. That's right. *Know* it! Don't get caught in a trap of taking on the roles and responsibilities of your mate until they "get themselves together," or because "somebody's gotta do it or it won't get done."

If your mate can't carry their load in the relationship, you'd better find out now rather than after you get married. If your relationship can't bear life's load without you having to carry it while your mate gets their self together (whatever that means), *leave*—and let the chips fall where they may. Otherwise...and trust me...you are setting yourself up for months, or even years, of frustratingly inconsistent and unpredictable high and lows in your relationship.

My wife and I were coaching a married couple in our Family Bootcamp who was in this situation. Andre and Kayden, we'll call them, are a blended family of eight. He had two, she had two, and they had two children together. Their roles were completely reversed. Kayden was responsible for leading the family. She did all the purpose and task-oriented planning. Even the little task-oriented planning Andre did, she had go behind him and make sure it was done right because he often didn't take into consideration key factors that were fundamentally basic to her.

This led to years of frustration for the both of them. Kayden always felt like she was the parent and Andre was her seventh child. His self-esteem was shot! He always felt like she was second-guessing him, and that she didn't trust nor respect him. There was a constant back and forth power struggle between his God-given authority and her experientially proven leadership in running the family.

Over the years, they tried and tried to reverse the roles. Kayden would fall back and give Andre the reins to the family. But some of his decisions would eventually steer the wagon off the road— even to the point of losing their house, car, and jobs. Then she would step back in to right the carriage. This cycle went on for two years before they asked us for help. And it continued for some time while working with us. Eventually Kayden resolved that she would have to maintain the reins of the family if they were going to stay married and prosper.

Their fight to reverse the order in their marriage was hard and long. They ultimately got a divorce.

Now, I know some women are probably saying to themselves, "I'd be outta there!" Well...that's why they came to the Family Bootcamp: to get help and avoid separation if possible.

Andre really wanted to reverse the roles and responsibilities in his family and assume the leadership role. But his inability to lead, poor judgment, and bad decision-making created such distrust in his wife that she felt more secure at the helm running things herself.

What greatly concerned me was the perception their children would have of marriage, and how that would affect their future relationships. Will their daughters grow up with the same distrust of men, thinking that women have to run everything in order for the family to be secure? Will their sons grow up thinking they can do whatever they want with their money because *she* will take care of it?

Practice Operating in Your Roles

As you are getting to know each other, practice operating in your assigned roles. Start with small things like planning task-oriented activities and events. Now be mindful, this is practice. Guys, don't call it quits the first time she starts grabbing the reins and trying to run things. Ladies, don't throw in the towel at the first horrible decision he makes that negatively affects you.

Look for patterns of behavior. That's the giveaway. If he or she commits to change, but continues with the same pattern of behavior, be concerned. If their patterns continue over time, lay down some ultimatums for when their behavior must change in order to continue in this relationship (and that timeframe should be a generous length of time). If ultimatums don't influence change to your satisfaction, then fellas, get your hat. Ladies, get your purse. And get thee gone!

Yes, this is a tough stance. But your future happiness or misery is what you're gambling with. If he or she cares enough about you, then they should be willing to change—over time.

Even if you feel they care about you, and they're willing to change...but don't, leave anyway. When you are in the middle of a frustratingly chaotic power struggle, you won't be thinking, "...but he/she really cares about me!"

The fact is, you won't care how much they care about you! All you'll care about is why he won't get off his blankety-blank and get moving; or why she won't shut the blankety-blank up and leave you the heck alone!

The best of intentions of past actions are always trumped by present feelings of hurt, disgust, disappointment, disrespect, and frustration. So I say again, get thee gone!

Now I know some of you will agree that you should leave...but you'll end up staying in the relationship anyway. I'm confident this will happen again because sometimes people make decisions that are contrary to their own betterment. Their decision-making process is heavily influenced by their emotions.

This emotional decision-making behavior is both a blessing and a curse. In later chapters, I will explain to you why some people make stupid emotional decisions that cripple and destroy you, or your relationships. Then I'll teach you how to use those same emotions to make wise decisions, which will propel you toward accomplishing common goals together with your partner.

God-Given Selection

But while I was watching Bernie, unbeknownst to me, she was watching me too. She watched me purge my tomfoolery and hijinks ways and replace them with a new, God-fearing lifestyle. She respected my opinion. She began asking my advice on serious matters in her life. She saw that my words matched my actions and that I could be trusted to do exactly what I said was going to do—not just for her but in all areas of my life. She noticed that I obtained some qualities that would make for a good husband in her eyes.

September 1996 arrived. There were still three women on the list. I had to make the decision. I asked some of the married men I respected at the church how they knew that their wife was "the one." They all said the same thing: "You'll just know." Well, that helped! It was now the middle of September. And this was the most important decision I had ever made in my life. So I prayed about it.

Finally the Lord answered my prayers. A series of interactions caused two to lose favor with me, but Bernie and I were steadily growing closer and closer. Then, one day I looked up and the woman of my dreams had been sitting right next to me at work for the past two years.

The only thing I had to do next was convince her to marry me. So one Saturday afternoon, I called and told her to get dressed because I was coming over to pick her up. I had to go over my mom's house to wash clothes and I wanted her to come with me (hey...I didn't have a washer or dryer in my house back then).

She reluctantly agreed. On my way to my mom's house, we stopped by my dad's house just to say hi. I introduced her to my dad. Then we left and went to meet my mother. That was the first and only time I have ever introduced my parents to any woman since my high school girlfriend.

While I was washing clothes, I was hungry and I knew she was hungry too. "Come on. Let's go get something to eat. I haven't fed you yet," I said nonchalantly. She had a puzzled look on her face that seemed to say, "When has it been your responsibility to feed me?" But she dared not say anything and mess up a free meal. So I took her out for dinner.

While we were eating, I felt like I was standing outside a double-dutch rope trying to figure out when to jump in and tell her that she's the one. Finally I saw an opening. She started talking about wanting to look for a job in our Fort Worth, Texas facility so she could be closer to her mother in California.

"You can't do that," I said all cool, calm, and collected.

"Why?" she asked as she looked up with a puzzled look on her face.

"Because you're the one. You're the one I want. I've prayed about it. And you're the one I want."

She's frozen.

She knew about my plan. She knew about my timeline. And she saw me transform into being a man of my word. So if I said something, she knew I meant it.

"Now I'm not asking you to marry me right now," I continued. "That's too much for you to handle. But I am letting you know my intentions to enter into a relationship with you that leads toward marriage."

She's still frozen. And she knew I wasn't playing. She knew about my plan. She knew about my timeline. And she saw me transform into being a man of my word. So if I said something, she knew I meant it.

Suddenly she started looking all around the restaurant, under the table, behind her, and around corners. Then blurted out, "Okay, where's the camera? Oprah? Montel? Where are they? Where's the camera? You're kidding, right?"

I burst out laughing. Because she was seriously looking all over the restaurant for the camera crew to come running down the aisle like on Punk'd.

"No. I'm serious. You're the one I want. I love you."

That's when she knew I was serious. And that's when she also got terrified. Because she knew our relationship was about to change forever. She was speechless and she couldn't eat anymore. So we packed up her food and went to pick up my clothes from my mom's house before I took her home.

In the following week, we underwent daily rounds of intense discussion. Although we knew each other, we had never talked to each other with the intentions of marrying one another. Our talks were more like negotiations about what we each wanted.

expected, and required in a relationship.

Exactly one week later, Saturday, September 28, I was heading over to Bernie's apartment, listening to a tape by Louis Greenup about fathers handing their daughters over in marriage to men who aren't qualified for marriage. He was making the analogy that handing your daughter over to a man that has not been properly trained to be a husband is like allowing her to get on a plane with a pilot that has not been trained to fly. I found the analogy interesting, given where I was in my life at the time.

When I arrived at Bernie's apartment, I told Bernie about the message I was listening to. When I finished, she looked directly at me and very deliberately asked, "Do you know how to fly the plane?"

"Yes. I'm just waiting on the co-pilot." I quickly replied.

She paused for a moment. "Okay. Let's do it."

Within the course of one week, we went from being close friends and co-workers, having never dated one another, to being engaged to be married. One year later, we were married on October 10, 1997.

Chapter 4:

How to Find Out the Common Goal for Your Marriage

With all this attention being placed on accomplishing the common goals of your relationship, the question remains, "How do I find out what the common goal is?" Fair question.

But let me first warn you, you might not like the path we are about to venture down. You might feel like Luke Skywalker on a journey to find the Force. In Star Wars, everybody was pulling for the young Jedi-in-training to come into the fullness of power that resided in him. But if you ask Mr. Skywalker if he enjoyed the process to come into the fullness of his power, he might have had a few choice words for you. And that's because within every answer of "what," there precedes the question of "how."

In order for Luke Skywalker to become a Jedi (what), he had to go through the Jedi training process (how). Before you can become a legal driver (what), you have to go to driving school to learn (how) to drive. Before Jesus could become the sacrificial Lamb of God and savior of the world (what), he had to go through the wilderness, assassination attempts, backstabbing, persecution, and death (how).

So erase any notion of finding out 'what' God has determined your common goal to be without going through the 'how' in order to find out. It just doesn't work like that.

Abraham went that route. Abraham's first born son Ishmael was born through his wife's maid-servant Hagar instead of with his wife Sarah, the one God told him would bear his son. I'll spare you the details. But let's just say they had some "Real Housewives of Canaan" type of baby mama drama up in that house.

I also tried fending for self too. I had a go-it-alone strategy that didn't work. As I mentioned in the introduction, I planned my career down to a T. Well, after several failed businesses, thousands of dollars spent, and seven years of waiting, I finally discovered the Wiggins Household's common goal at age 30. It was to rule over my marriage by exhibiting Christian principles that can be used as an example for others to follow; and subdue families on the brink of divorce by teaching husbands and wives how to make their marriage work by using the same Christian principles I used in my marriage. You're reading our common goal right now.

Finding Out Your Individual Purpose

Before you can discover the common goal in your relationship, you first have to discover who you are and what your purpose is. What do you bring to the table?

God laid out the blueprint for discovering your purpose in two separate excerpts of scripture in the books of Romans and James.

Romans 12

The book of Romans is the Apostle Paul's letter to the church in Rome, Italy, which included both Jews and non-Jews, called Gentiles. Socially, Jews and Gentiles had a little beef with each other. Some Jews had too much pride in themselves because they were God's chosen people and the Gentiles were not. And true to form, some of this conflict made its way into the church in Rome.

In the first 10 chapters of Paul's letter to the Roman church, Paul addressed some of these problematic issues:

sin, righteousness, and the belief in gospel of Jesus Christ. But in chapter 11, he was explaining to the Jewish people how God showed mercy to the Gentiles by giving them the same rights and privileges that were once reserved exclusively for the Jews. So he urged them to treat Gentiles like brothers instead of acting like they were better than them.

We pick it up in the beginning of chapter 12 with Paul now focusing on the Gentiles.

"Therefore, I urge you, brothers, in view of God's mercy, to offer your bodies as living sacrifices, holy and pleasing to God—this is your spiritual act of worship. Do not conform any longer to the pattern of this world, but be transformed by the renewing of your mind. Then you will be able to test and approve what God's will is—his good, pleasing and perfect will." (Romans 12:1-2)

Because God showed mercy to Gentiles by giving them the same salvation, grace, rights, and privileges as His chosen people, the Jews, we should make the sacrifice to present ourselves to God as holy and acceptable according to His standards. This is how we are to worship God. We should also stop conforming to the ways of world, because we don't belong to the world anymore. We belong to God now. Instead, we should be transformed from the ways of the world by renewing our thinking.

Paul says we should show our gratitude for God's mercy in one of two ways: we should 1) present our bodies to God as holy and acceptable by God, and 2) transform our thinking.

Paul then adds a third way in the latter part of verse two that is critical to finding out your common goal.

He writes, "...*Then you will be able to test and approve what God's will is—his good, pleasing and perfect will.*"

STOP THE PRESSES! There's the answer to finding out your purpose!

Paul tells us that by aligning the way you think to the way God thinks, you will be able to test God's ways against the world's ways. And after you have tested them, you will be able to see and approve what God's will is [for you]. And His will is good, acceptable, and perfect.

Finding out your purpose in life relies on you taking this very important test, where you test your own beliefs, thinking, and actions against what God wants you to believe, think, and act.

He's essentially telling you, "Go ahead. Test me!" Because He knows at the end of the day, His way will to prove to be the best way for you—even if you can't see it in the beginning.

This testing-and-approving process for finding out what is truth versus what is not isn't unique to the Christian faith. If you've ever had to do a science project or written a research paper in school, then you're familiar with this test-and-approve methodology. It's used by scientists, researchers, clinicians, and Jedis! Yes, Jedis! The process for finding your purpose is the same process Jedi-master Yoda used on our famed hero, Luke Skywalker.

The Testing and Approving of a Jedi

In Star Wars Episode V: The Empire Strikes Back, young and naive Luke Skywalker knew about the power of the Force. His destiny lay in using the Force. But in spite of his own efforts, he couldn't seem to muster the power of the Force on his own. At first, he tried to acquire it his own way. But to no avail.

He didn't find the right path until he crash-landed his X-Wing Starfighter on Dagobah and met up with Yoda, a Jedi master. Master Yoda patiently walked Luke through a rigorous training process. He challenged Luke to get rid of his current beliefs, thought patterns, and actions and tap into the power of the Force, which resided in him. He had to believe, think, and act like a Jedi.

Luke had a breakthrough when he pushed pass his own mental blockade, tapped into the Force and was able to move his crashed X-Wing Starfighter telepathically. Luke finally understood what Yoda was trying to teach him. He went on to master the power of the Force to (spoiler alert!!!) defeat Darth Vader in the final showdown.

In order for Luke Skywalker to get the "what" (the Force), he had to go through the "how," the Yoda-Jedi crucible.

And the Apostle Paul was making the same point. In order for you to know *what* God's purpose is for you, you have to go through your own crucible, which is 1) presenting your body to God as holy and acceptable, 2) transforming your thinking, and 3) testing God's ways against the world's ways. And after the test, you will 4) approve that God's ways are good, acceptable, and perfect.

Presenting Your Body as Holy and Acceptable

This is the easiest part. All you have to do is acknowledge that you are neither holy nor acceptable to God, for you are saturated with conformity to the way the world does things.

Therefore, present your body to the Lord. Swap out your beliefs of what's right and wrong and replace them with the Lord's standards of what's right and wrong. Trade in your plans for how you live your life for His plans of how you *should* live your life. And change your behavior to what would be considered pleasing and acceptable to God by his standards…not yours.

At this juncture, it's all about accepting God's ways over the world's ways. It's not about whether you have sinned or not sinned. That's not the question, nor the issue God wants you to focus on.

Renewing Your Mind

Transforming your thinking, or renewing your mind, is also easy. It goes hand-in-glove with following God's ways. Authors Walvoord and Zuck wrote in their commentary on Romans that the key to this change is in the mind.[11] For that is the control center of one's attitudes, thoughts, feelings, and actions.

Renewal takes place by reading and studying scripture, praying, and fellowshipping with like-minded people on a continual basis. The intent is for this to become a habit, until it becomes a behavior and then into a lifestyle.

Luke Skywalker didn't have a Jedi manual to follow, like we do the Bible. But he did have to meditate on his new belief system, and he modified his behavior, which could loosely be correlated to studying or praying. He also had Yoda, a like-minded Jedi master to hang out with. That proved most beneficial. It's like having Jesus as your own private spiritual sensei.

---

[11] Walvoord and Zuck (1983)

God's Test Taking Process: The Testing of Your Faith

Now the third part, testing God's ways versus the world's way is where it gets really tricky. Unless you were an academic savant in school, you probably weren't too fond of test-taking time. Or maybe you were, because you studied and were prepared. But if you were like me, a strong C+ student in high school and a strong B student in undergrad, test-taking time was usually met with some anxiety.

Regardless of your previous test-taking anxiety thresholds, God's test-taking process trumps all other testing experiences hands-down.

Staying in the New Testament, we are going to jump to another book in the Bible written by James the Just, as he was called (Jesus' brother).

James Chapter 1

After Jesus' death, the governing authorities wanted to kill anyone who still followed the ways of Jesus, known back then as "The Way." That sent followers into exile, scattered throughout the entire region. Now, the 12 tribes of

Israel, who were actually the 12 sons of Jacob from the Old Testament, and their lineage (Jacob's name was later changed by God to Israel, hence the 12 tribes of Israel), were scattered throughout the world by the Assyrian army.

During this time, the church was formed by both Jews and Gentiles who still followed The Way. However, the church had to meet secretly in the homes of faithful followers of Jesus. James the Just was a leader in one of those churches.

In the opening part of his letter, James starts with a greeting to the 12 tribes dispersed throughout the land. Then he starts talking about tests.

"2 Consider it pure joy, my brothers, whenever you face trials of many kinds, 3 because you know that the testing of your faith develops perseverance. 4 Perseverance must finish its work so that you may be mature and complete, not lacking anything. 5 If any of you lacks wisdom, he should ask God, who gives generously to all without finding fault, and it will be given to him. 6 But when he asks, he must believe and not doubt, because he who doubts is like a wave of the sea, blown and tossed by the wind. 7

That man should not think he will receive anything from the Lord; 8 he is a double-minded man, unstable in all he does."

James introduces several topics in this passage, discussing "trials," "testing," "perseverance," and "wisdom." Each topic is discussed in multiple books throughout the Bible. However, James speaks to them all within the context of the 12 tribes dispersed throughout the land and the church being persecuted because of its belief in Jesus Christ.

Here's my paraphrased version of what James says in verses two through four: *Greetings to the believers in Jesus the Christ scattered throughout the land. You are indeed facing many kinds of trials right now because of your faith (i.e., what you believe). But I want you to look at these trials with joy. Because, know that...God uses these trials to test your faith. And you must have your faith tested by these kinds of trials because these tests of your faith produce perseverance. And you must be able to persevere in order for you to be mature and compete. And once you are mature and complete, you won't lack for anything.*

God's Testing Process

God's testing process includes trials designed to challenge your faith. That is, they test what you believe after you've been *"transformed by the renewing of your mind,"* taken from Roman 12:1.

When you were "conformed to the pattern of this world," you had your own belief system influenced by the world's way of thinking. But Paul is asking you to trade in the world's way of thinking for God's way of thinking.

This new way of thinking isn't something you can get on your own. God has to give it to you. But once He gives it to you, He begins to test you to see if it's authentic by sending you through different trials.

So those issues you have been going through, or those people and problems that have been bothering you? Yes, those are trials. That issue that keeps coming up in your life over and over again? Yes, that's perseverance. And that problem you used to struggle with, but now have overcome? Yes, that's maturity and completeness. It's God's testing process.

True to form, once you become mature and complete in that area, you will not lack anything. Because you will have the experience and proficiency at handling anything that comes up.

It's Going to Take Time

Inherent in God's testing process is an element that I didn't include in the list above...time. So let me set your expectations now. This indefinite amount of test-taking time makes taking the test so unpredictable and unpleasant. I mean, really, who wants to take a test where the proctor says, "The test will begin now and I will let you know when it's over. Begin!"

That's like when I was working with a personal trainer and he told me to start doing pushups and didn't tell me how many to do. At least if I knew how many to do, or how long to do them, I'd be able to mentally prepare for it.

So I had to approach those pushups like James commanded, "Consider it pure joy..." because these pushups were testing my mental and physical perseverance. And after I persevered with these pushups, I will be cock-diesel and strong, able to lift anything...well, okay, maybe not anything.

Young master Skywalker would concur too. When he was facing trials during his Yoda-Jedi crucible, he didn't just past one test and then scurry on his way. No, Yoda put him through several tests to make sure he really knew how to persevere. He never knew how long his training was going to be. Only after he demonstrated that he could persevere through trials of many kinds was he able to leave Dagobah.

And as James the Just encouraged the 12 Tribes, Luke Skywalker should have very well "considered it pure joy" that he faced those many kinds of trials before his ultimate showdown with Darth Vader. Otherwise, Luke would have met Darth Vader still doubting his own ability to persevere and defeat him. And that is what James went on to address in verses five through eight.

Ask God If You Need Help

He ended verse four stating that, *"you may be mature and complete, not lacking anything."* He picks up at verse five, *"If any of you lacks wisdom, he should ask God, who gives generously to all without finding fault, and it will be given to him."*

How can he say you will not lack anything in one verse and then start the very next verse by saying, "*If any of you lacks wisdom...*"? Is this a contradiction? No, it's a compliment. James understands that you need help during these times of testing, so he's suggesting that you ask God for it.

Now this wisdom he's talking about is more than just knowledge or know-how. It may take on different forms depending on the situation. But this wisdom is God-given understanding, God-inspired wisdom that comes from Him, not man-derived. And He freely distributes this wisdom generously to believers who ask for it.

Even though we're not perfect and we have faults, and don't do everything right, God still generously gives us wisdom without condemning us. He does not require that we "get right with" Him first or perform a bunch of good deeds to offset the bad ones before we can ask for His wisdom. This is a source of great joy for those of us who are not perfect...I know it is for me.

...But Don't Doubt What You Once Believed

Whereas the fifth verse of James was complementary, these next two verses are a caveat and are the hinge that validates everything James said up to this point. He writes, "*6 But when he asks, he must believe and not doubt, because he who doubts is like a wave of the sea, blown and tossed by the wind. 7 That man should not think he will receive anything from the Lord; 8 he is a double-minded man, unstable in all he does.*"

It is an egregious thing to be given special responsibilities and the wisdom to carry it out, and then shirk from it when called upon because you doubt your ability. For this reason, you shouldn't expect to receive anything from the Lord because you can't be trusted.

So whenever you ask for wisdom from God, you better ask according to your faith. Because asking for something from God and then doubting that He can or will give it to you is really an indictment against you, not against God.

For example, let's say you're dating someone. And you've gone through a bunch of trials with your (now) friend. You are at the point where it's time to either take it to the next level of commitment or start pulling back. So you pray and asked God for the wisdom to determine if she's the right person for you. And some time later, you get a feeling that she's a good person for you. And you believe that answer came from God, because you prayed about it.

But a couple days later, all sorts of doubt creeps in your mind. "Was that really God? How can I be sure? Maybe I should ask my boys. Or maybe I should start dating other women just to see if there's anyone else out there better than her." You have essentially doubted your way off the faith upon which you once stood.

James likened this to being waves of the sea being tossed to and fro by the winds. You are a double-minded man. Proclaiming, "I believe" today and then tomorrow "I don't believe." Your faith provides your life no stability, not just in one area, but in every area.

God does not want you to be so spiritually wishy-washy with the wisdom He gives you. That's why James says such a person should not expect to receive anything from the Lord.

Summary

This entire testing process is the third and final step in finding out your purpose. Remember, the first two steps, identified in Romans 12, were to present your body as holy and acceptable and renew your mind. This last step was to test and approve what God's good, pleasing, and acceptable will is. And God's testing process, outlined in James, involves you facing trials of many kinds.

As you face them, consider it a joyful occasion. These trials are really God testing your faith. And your faith must be tested so that you may endure and persevere. While your faith is being tested, feel free to ask God for wisdom on how to make it through them. He'll provide it to you without requiring you to get everything right and be the perfect Christian. But when you ask, make sure you ask according to faith, what you believe God can and will do.

Didn't I tell you testing God's process is tricky? Without knowing this very involved testing process, it's no wonder why divorce has hovered between 40%-50% since 1980, and people are waiting to get married later than ever before.

As you can tell, marriage is not for the weak at heart. It takes a lot of work to be happily married.

If you've found someone with whom you're willing to put in this hard work, then you're at a good starting point to create a happy, loving, trusting relationship.

Part 2:

Four Steps to Providing Leadership in Your Relationship—Initiate, Communicate, Execute, and Check-in

Everything you've read so far was to prepare you for what you need to know about leadership and relationships. Consider it the free dinner rolls and glass of water you get at a restaurant. Now, you're about to get scuba-diving deep into the waters of relationships, leadership, power, influence, and decision-making.

Up to this point, you've learned what leadership is, what leadership looks like in the context of an organizationally structured relationship, and how to prepare yourself to carry out your roles and responsibilities. But knowing what leadership *is* and knowing how to *provide* leadership are two different things. A man, for example, may know and understand that he should use good communication skills with his mate. But if he doesn't actually know how to do it or doesn't know how to do it with the person he's currently with, that won't do him any good.

It's like a Musketeer going to battle with the best crafted sword but was never trained how to use it. Call the coroner!

For the remainder of this book, I will be teaching you a specific leadership model that is different from the kind of leadership you might have used at work, school, the military, or a volunteer organization. So I must warn you: this will challenge your whole perspective about leadership.

This book was written to men and for men. However, women should also pay close attention to this section too, especially unmarried women. While married women can benefit from this section to understand how to best help their husband become a better leader, unmarried women can use this model of leadership as the litmus test by which to assess any potential suitor's leadership ability.

I.C.E.C. Leadership Model

This leadership model is made up of four sequential steps: Initiate, Communicate, Execute, and Check-in, or I.C.E.C.

I created the I.C.E.C. leadership model from extensive research in leadership theory, principles, and

> **I.C.E.C Leadership Model**
> - Initiate
> - Communicate
> - Execute
> - Check-in

application; sound biblical theology; human behavioral sciences best practices, couples therapy principles and application, and neurological science, combined with 15 years of experience consulting with couples, and 17 years of marriage.

All these theories, principles, and experiences were put in a blender and mixed into the perfect leadership cocktail to teach men how to become the Christian man his woman will trust, respect, and actually want to follow.

God-Given Marriage

Seventeen years later, we are still best friends. I still love her, and she loves me. We've had ups and downs, like every couple. I'm not the perfect husband and she's not the perfect wife. We argue about everyday life issues. One ground-breaking argument we had was about two months after the honeymoon. Bernie was extremely upset with me because she felt that I wasn't pulling my fair share of the load.

See, during our week long pre-marital negotiation period, we talked about what our roles and responsibilities would be. Because I didn't like cooking, we decided that she would do the cooking. She didn't like driving, so I did all the driving. And so on.

Well, one day, Bernie was cooking dinner after working nine hours. Rightfully so, she didn't feel like cooking that night. Furthermore, she was getting frustrated because I was sitting in the man-spot on the couch (directly in front of the TV) with the remote in one hand and a can of soda in the other, waiting patiently for my beautiful new wife to bring me a tray of freshly prepared dinner. After we ate dinner, I put my dishes in the sink and returned to the man-spot on the couch. That's when she hit the fan. I don't remember everything she said, but it sound something like this:

"Blah blah blah...I'm doing too much!"
"Blah blah blah...I'm tired!"
"Blah blah blah...cook dinner every night!"
"Blah blah blah...all you do is sit in front of the TV with a remote in your hand!"

"Blah blah blah...you expect me to clean the dishes!"
"Blah blah blah...it's not fair!"
"Blah blah blah...you don't do anything!"

Taken aback, I truly was not prepared for this level of heatedness, especially after a full belly. But something she said got me a little heated too. Granted, she had some valid points, which we later renegotiated. But saying I "don't do anything" really upset me. What that meant to me was she didn't appreciated nor respected my contribution to our marriage. It was like all the work I was doing to try and make our marriage work was disregarded.

The more we argued, the more heated we both got. And it became clearer to me that she really didn't know what my contribution was to our marriage. Because...every day after work she had to cook and do the dishes, and all I had to do was drive us to work and to church...she felt she was getting the short end of the stick. And it was affecting how she felt about me and our marriage. This was a major crisis in the newly formed Wiggins Household.

It was at that moment, standing in my kitchen, in month two of our marriage, I got a serious hint of what leadership is in a marriage. Although it may have seemed to Bernie that I wasn't doing anything, I realized what I was doing was providing leadership to my household. But, I didn't even recognize it as such. And Bernie didn't recognize it either.

Chapter 5:
Step 1: Initiate

Initiating Structure: The Leadership Theory

Initiating Structure

In order for this I.C.E.C Leadership Model to work in your relationship, it can't be just based on my opinion or my own experiences of how I provide leadership in my relationship. It must be anchored in sound leadership theories that have been proven reliable through the test of time. So let's start there.

George Homans was a leadership theorist that was one of the first to study the actions, relationships, and beliefs of small groups. He introduced a new method of analysis and influential theories on group dynamics. Homans identified a leader of a group as one *who originates the interaction of the group.*[12]

John Hemphill's research expanded upon Homans' definition of a leader as one who *initiates structure in the*

---

[12] Homans, 1950

interaction as part of the process for solving a mutual problem.[13]

These two researchers connected two key leadership theories: 1) interaction between members within a group and 2) initiating the structure of the interaction within a group.

"Initiating structure" is a technical way of saying, "defining the roles and responsibilities of the members within a group."

But initiating structure by itself is not leadership. It's only part of it. In my pickup basketball game analogy, I initiated structure and by default I was the leader because I created the roles on my team. I'm the point guard, one man is the center, another is the forward, and so on. But once the game started, Mr. Hot-Hands was clearly the leader on the court because he was the one running everything. And that highlights a gap in this early leadership theory.

Maintaining Structure (Roles)

And Stogdill realized that too.[14] That's why he later added an important concept called "maintenance" to the

---

[13] Hemphill, 1954

initiating structure theory. Maintenance says, *the one who creates and "maintains" the roles within a group is actually the leader*.

According to Dr. Bernard Bass, the most influential leader in leadership research, maintaining roles consists of maintaining standards, meeting deadlines, and deciding what will be done and how.[15] Maintaining roles involves the leader establishing clear patterns and lines of communication that facilitate, not impede, the task being accomplished.

Individuals who initially create roles but then hesitate to take initiative, make suggestions only when asked, or let other members of the group pursue a goal the way they think best...lose their mantle of leadership to the one who can better guide the group in solving a problem or achieving a goal.

Initiating Roles in Organizationally Structured Relationships

The person who provides leadership is responsible for initiating the roles for their relationship. But before any

---

[14] Stogdill, 1959
[15] Bass, 2008

roles can be initiated, there must begin a common goal (either task-oriented or purpose-oriented) or a problem to solve. Otherwise, how can a leader assign a role to accomplish something without knowing what that something is?

For example, a couple must first know it's going to tackle a weekend project of painting the living room before the leader can assign roles of who is responsible for what.

Know the Scope of the Common Goal

But knowing the common goal isn't enough. The leader must also understand the scope of the common goal in order to initiate the appropriate roles.

With the example of painting a living room, there are lots of decisions to be made in order to accomplish the goal. You just don't stick a roller in a paint tray and start rolling paint on the walls. What color are you going to paint the walls? What finish are you going to use: flat, eggshell or satin? What color and finish is currently on your walls? This will determine if you'll need to use a primer and how many coats of primer. What kind of rollers and brushes are you going to use? Do you need to repair any damage to the wall before you paint? Are you going to tape the ceiling, baseboards, and molding or paint free-hand?

If you don't get a grasp of the scope of the common goal, it will cause you problems in the future.

After the scope of the project has been fleshed out, then the leader can initiate structure by assigning roles and responsibilities. Who's going to repair the wall damage? Who's going to tape the ceiling and molding? Who's going to cut-in the corners and who's going to paint the surface of the walls? And most importantly, what kind of pizza are you going to order?

Interaction During Task-Oriented Goals is Necessary Before Pursuing Purpose-Oriented Goals

Grasping the scope of projects like this might seem quite daunting for some. But working through these kinds of task-oriented goals and solving the myriad of problems that arise while doing so is a necessary evil for relationships. Why? Because couples need to experience success interacting with each other while working through trivial task-oriented activities like painting a living room before they can move on to the more important purpose-oriented decisions, like whether to adopt a child.

Purpose-oriented decisions are related to the purpose for which you were created and the purpose for which the two of you were brought together. The purpose-oriented decisions tie directly to what you as a couple will do to fill, rule, and subdue.

And true to form, just like He did with his son, God is not going to trust you with the rich purposeful intentions of His kingdom without first testing you to see if you and your relationship can hack it. You have to first show and prove that your relationship has the perseverance to withstand the problems associated with rudimentary task-oriented projects.

Some marriages can't weather these small tests without falling into a death-spiral tailspin after only a few months together, as evidenced by a famous socialite who was only married for 10 weeks before filing for divorce. Examples like these highlight the importance of perseverance.

Troubleshooting task-oriented goals forces you, as a couple, to work through situations and feelings, and force you to deal with your own prejudices, selfish ambitions, presuppositions, and work out a solution between two opposing views.

If you've ever tried to come to an agreement on an issue where each of you dug in to your own positions not wanting to budge an inch or show the slightest hint of weakness, then you're right where God wants you. For it's in that place where God wanted to see what you will do to resolve the issue. How did you work through your differences and come to a solution?

If you can't figure out these simple task-oriented problems, then how do you expect to solve the problems that will surely arise in the plan He has for you to fill, subdue, and rule the earth? You won't.

So embrace all of the task-oriented goals put before you. Don't shirk from them. But with expanded stride, hasten toward them. And know, it's not about getting everything right the first time because you probably won't get it right the first time. When you were a baby, you didn't walk without falling the first time. Now look at you, walking everyday without falling. Congratulations. How'd you do it? You tried. Failed. Then tried again. In other words, you persevered. Follow the same approach in solving problems and working through task-oriented issues in your relationship.

Interaction During Task-Oriented Goals Helps Relationships Learn How to Work Together

As the two of you interact and work your way through solving problems and striving to accomplish random task-oriented goals, success is achieved through conflict. You will experience problems, difficulty, failures, stresses, and all manner of adverse circumstance.

Tuckman refers to this mandatory stage of relationships as the storming stage, because varying ideas for solving problems and accomplishing goals roll in like a fast moving thunderstorm.[16] And this is the stage that every relationship must go through to be successful.

Interacting with one another through this monsoon of problem solving is where you find that sweet spot. That is, that optimal relational dynamic that allows you to interact in a positive productive manner while tackling whatever problem or task-oriented goal lies before you.

Behavior patterns become normalized. You figure out what works and learn how to avoid what doesn't. You understand your individual role and responsibilities. You

---

[16] Tuckman, 1965

know where both of you fit in the larger scheme of things. You know how to better manage resources. You learn how each person processes information and makes decisions.

Interaction During Task-Oriented Goals Reveals Who Should Take on What Roles

You also find out each person's strengths and weaknesses. One person might be very detailed while the other person is more big picture. My wife is the detailed person and I'm Mr. Big Picture. One person may be very strategic in their thinking ("What's the overall plan for painting the living room?"), while the other person is more itemized in their thinking ("What's the next step in order to finish painting this living room?").

Neither is right or wrong. Whoever takes the responsibility of initiating roles for a task, that person will likely emerge as the leader. I say "likely" because as I stated above, you have to maintain the roles in the group in order to continue as the leader.

Admittedly, this is a simplified look at how the leadership theory of initiating roles works. But that's intentional. Because when you transfer this theory into a relationship context, specifically a Christian organizationally structured relationship, leadership roles become more defined: he has a specific role and she has a specific role.

Men & Leadership in Relationships

Up to this point, I've only been speaking about initiating roles in a non-gender specific context. That's because leadership is not person-specific. Anyone can serve as a leader. He can be a leader or she can be a leader.

However, when you enter the confines of the biblical structure of how a marital relationship was designed by the Creator, the role of leader has been delegated to the male.

Remember, in the first two chapters of Genesis, God gave the common goal of filling, subduing, and ruling to both man and woman. But he put man in the garden first and gave him the responsibility to initiate roles. [*"...He brought them to the man to see what he would name them; and whatever the man called each living creature, that was its name." (Genesis 2:18)*]. Adam named the animals, worked the field, and cultivated the ground.

Even when woman showed up on the scene after a good night's sleep, he initiated structure and created her role. It's actually hilarious to me how it all went down. Adam wakes up from a good night's sleep and before him stands a naked woman. Up until now, he's seen nothing but plants and animals. The first thing he says is, "*This...*" (did he just call her a "this"?) "*...is now bone of my bones and flesh of my flesh; she shall be called woman, for she was taken out of man*" (Genesis 2:23).

Adam initiated structure by creating her role. He recognized she had the same bones structure and flesh he had. What he first referred to as "*this,*" he now referred to as "she."

Oh the simplicity of it all. Adam was the leader, and Eve was the perfect suitable helper for him. Their roles were established and clear.

But it didn't stay that way for long. As Bass correctly assessed, maintaining your role is necessary if you are to maintain leadership. Adam failed to do that when he allowed Eve to lead him into eating the fruit of the tree from which God told him not to eat. And we all know what happened next.

Men, you are the one responsible for being the leader in a marriage. And that leadership begins by initiating and maintaining roles when pursuing a task-oriented goal. In a marriage, leadership is yours by birthright. It was assigned to you by the Father. You can't delegate it to your wife. You do not have delegating authority.

Are Some Wives Better Leaders Than Their Husbands?

However, you can abdicate it, like Adam did. You can also neglect it or refuse to acknowledge it. These are some of the reasons why women end up taking over the reins of many households and becoming the leader.

Research has clearly shown that among American families, women are predominantly the ones leading the way. In a 2009 CNN and Time magazine poll[17], women are reported as the ones who take on more responsibilities for the home and family than their male partners. Women were noted as the ones primarily responsible for child care, managing family finances, and making purchasing decisions.

---

[17] Gibbs, 2009

At an increasing rate, women are proving to be better at leading families than their men. This is not a slight against all men. It's a credit to these women. Women are designed to be suitable helpers. They are skilled with the aptitude to process a wide array of inputs and make decisions that helps the family accomplish its goals. This is an innate leadership quality. That is why women are proving to be equally successful when these skills and abilities are transferred to the male-dominated workplace.

But with respect to relationships, it's a natural inclination for women to care for the children, manage the budget, and make buying decisions for the family. If it will help their family and relationship, then it's a no-brainer for women to try to figure out how to solve a problem or accomplish a family goal, then do whatever it takes to make it happen.

Some Men Don't Lead

For whatever reasons, the same research shows men are increasingly failing to provide the necessary leadership. Some men in relationships aren't initiating roles to attempt to solve the problems. And they don't initiate roles for the many task-oriented goals the relationship undertakes.

Granted, there may be very valid reasons: he was never taught how, he was taught incorrectly, or what he was taught doesn't work in his current relationship with this woman. He might even be overwhelmed and struggles with making the right or timely decisions.

But some men are just plain apathetic. They don't have any input into whatever is going on in the relationship. He primarily relies on his woman to decide what the couple will do, when, and how they're going to do it. They just react, instead of proactively initiating a plan. This male absenteeism is very taxing on the woman and the relationship. Even though the woman has the capability to step in, step up, take the reins, and run things, God's structure for relationships was not designed to be manned by one person. Both parties need to be actively engaged in carrying out their roles and responsibilities.

So it's critical that men seize the opportunity of leadership and begin initiating roles for problems that arise and in task-oriented goals they want to accomplish.

Some Men are Leaders, but Bad Ones

Another thing some men can do to their leadership birthright is abuse it. In contrast to the absentee leader, there exists the man that is, in fact, a leader in his relationship, but he's a bad one.

"My Way" Man

There's the "My Way" Man. This man is overbearing, controlling, unyielding and insensitive to the cares or concerns of others. Everything has to be done his way or the woman will be met with quantum debates and arguments intended to persuade her to go with his way. He is uber-opinionated. Once he has his mind on something, no other reasonable solution or mountain of evidence to the contrary will sway him from his position. "I shall not be moved" is his battle call. Leadership in a relationship to him is, "Just do what I say and we'll be fine. Trust me."

The problem with "My Way" Man is that he expects trust that he has not earned, a blind trust of sorts. But he doesn't receive it because he puts little value in the opinions of his mate. In his mind, he does value her opinions and input, but to a very small degree and only in certain matters.

117

That's why he'll sometimes act like he's listening, so he won't appear rude or dismissive. But she can tell he's not really listening. And that's because he listened to as much as he deemed her input important. Because she doesn't feel valued, she doesn't trust or respect him, nor does she want to follow him.

"I Got This" Guy

Then there's the "I Got This" Guy. This guy claims he's got everything under control. He claims that he's taking care of business. Whenever a problem or situation arises, "I got this," he shouts, as if he's going to handle it. However, the fact is, he doesn't. He's got nothing. His "I got this" remedy only begets additional problems down the road.

For instance, when the "I Got This" Guy's mate tries to help him do some task-oriented project, like a good helpmate, or potential helpmate should, and asks, "Honey, have you considered doing it this way instead?" He pulls his "I got this" card out his pocket, effectively rejecting her help.

While some men can generally handle task-oriented issues as they arise, the "I Got This" Guy rejects offers of assistance because he wants to appear to be competently in control of that situation even though he isn't.

This stems from a man's insecurity about who he is and/or what he knows. No man *ever* wants to appear stupid in the eyes of his woman. No man *ever* wants to appear like he doesn't know what he's doing.

In Abraham Maslow's paper describing the five hierarchal needs that motivate human behavior[18], known as Maslow's hierarchy of needs, the fourth need he identified is a need for esteem, which is the feeling of self-esteem, competence, achievement, adequacy, accomplishment, and respect from others. This need is ordered right after man's need for belongingness and love, which he gets from being in a relationship. Although there is debate over the hierarchal sequence of the needs, research has proven the need for belongingness and love are a critical component of a man's happiness[19].

Maslow's theory confirms that if a man feels these things from his mate, then he will feel self-confident, have

---

[18] Maslow, 1943
[19] Tay, Deiner, 2011

119

high self-esteem, and be willing to cooperate with others while working on different tasks.

However, if he doesn't feel this esteem, then he will have feelings of incompetency, dread criticism, and resist any situation that brings his competency into question.

It's these feelings that lead him to mask any situation where he doesn't know what to do with, "I got this." It's his way of saying, "I don't know. I don't want to admit I don't know. I'll eventually figure it out. So leave me alone until I do."

But what inevitably happens is he takes the relationship on a rollercoaster while he experiments with solution after solution. If he would just admit he doesn't know and ask for help from his helpmate or potential helpmate, then the relationship would avoid the nausea brought on by his rollercoaster of emotional inadequacy.

"Don't Worry 'bout It" Dude

Similar to the "I Got This" Guy is the "Don't Worry 'bout It" Dude. "I Got This" Guy doesn't want to talk about solving a problem because he doesn't know how. But the "Don't Worry 'bout It" Dude doesn't want to talk about how to solve a problem because he just doesn't feel like talking about it.

He's that dude that is generally non-communicative. He keeps his thoughts to himself. He generally doesn't share his decisions, or how he came to his decision. He just decides what to do and does it. He's hard pressed to share his thoughts about any particular issue. But when pressed, he'll give some generic answer followed by, "Don't worry about it."

The problem with this style is that he is limiting his woman's participation in the decision- making process. Granted, some women like that their man can take charge and make decisions like that. That's a turn-on, especially for a woman who has an "I Got This" Guy.

But some women want to have more say in the decisions made in their relationship. It's a big deal to those who want to participate in the solutions. And if they feel omitted from the decision-making process, it sparks feelings of being controlled and manipulated. No woman flourishes in a relationship like that.

Even though the man may not be intentionally doing something that is causing him to be considered a bad leader, by not heeding his mate's request for more transparency and communication, he gives cause for such characterizations.

"I'm Sorry" Man

This man moves with purposeful intent. He is deliberate and decisive. However, when he makes decisions, he takes little-to-no care of the impact his actions will have on others in the relationship, or he fails to fully assess the impact before proceeding. Think of a bull in a china shop. And when the damage is done, he is shocked and confused how the carnage he left in his wake got there. That's when he hits you with the sad face and says, "I'm sorry."

Saying "I'm sorry" is the right thing to say when someone errs and makes a mistake. But what is wrong and egregious about "I'm Sorry" Man is his whole style is characterized by: think, act, wreck, apologize…repeat. That's not cool. The man leading this relationship constantly self-inflicts mayhem on the relationship and others in it, and then asks his woman to forgive him.

With every cyclical iteration, this man is shredding the trust and respect his woman has for him. He is effortlessly proving himself unreliable. Or should I say he is proving himself very reliable at causing havoc, misfortune, embarrassment, expensive mishaps, and a host of other hard-earned losses.

The woman in this man's life has grown to count on him causing reputable harm even when he doing nothing at all. Sometimes, it is his lack of doing something that causes damage. So he gets you coming *and* going.

On the surface, this behavior might appear to be due to lack of focus, laziness, insensitivity, or lack of attention to detail. However, some researchers believe that this behavior is linked to certain cognitive or neurological limitations, like dyslexia. Dyslexia is not a mental disorder. It just means that a person wasn't given that gift to process a whole lot information at one time. They process it differently. The Yale Center for Dyslexia & Creativity reports that more than 20% of the population is dyslexic, yet many go undiagnosed, untreated, and struggling with the effect of their dyslexia[20].

---

[20] The Yale Center for Dyslexia & Creativity

Depression is another potential reason why "I'm Sorry" Man keeps running afoul. Like "I Got This" Guy, he too wants to be esteemed, respected, and deemed as a "doer" by his woman. However, after a solid history of not being that guy, some men slip into a state of depression.

Depression is serious. Men suffering with depression need to go see a therapist or counselor who is trained to deal with this issue. It's not a matter of his boys punching him in his chest and yelling at him, "Man up!" Or his woman slapping him across his face and blurting out, "Be a man!" The effects of depression go so much deeper than those primitive remedies. But it will likely make matters worse.

Nonetheless, regardless if "I'm Sorry" Man is unfocused, lazy, insensitive, inattentive, or whether he's a bull in a china shop, the net effect of it all is he is a horrendous leader, and the woman in a relationship with him is suffering through it.

Adapt and Adjust

So if you are an unmarried woman and are dating someone like "My Way" Man, "I Got This" Guy, or "Don't Worry 'bout It" Dude, I hope you're not too deep into the relationship that you feel you can't walk away. Because you shouldn't marry him, at least not at this point of his maturation as a man. That's right! I said it and I meant it.

Sir, if you are any one of these types of leaders, your girlfriend or fiancé should not marry you because you are not ready for marriage yet. This may sound harsh or insensitive, even borderline disrespectful. But the reality is, if you get married while you are still a work in progress, her happiness will be solely contingent on 1) your *understanding* of what you need to change about yourself, 2) your *willingness* to do the uncomfortable work of making those changes, and 3) your *ability* to adapt and adjust your behavior accordingly, to create a new "normal."

Your understanding and willingness alone won't cut it. You must actually be *able* to make the changes in your behavior or else the culture of the relationship and the toxic environment in which it resides won't change.

Don't get me wrong, I'm not saying these changes have to be made overnight or have to happen all at once. That's impossible. But you'd better be taking some positive steps toward adapting and adjusting your behavior or else you're just giving lip service with no way to back it up.

So ladies, if you're currently dating or engaged to someone, make sure you are comfortable with his ability to adapt and adjust to relational differences. If you're not, I can nearly just about guarantee you will not be happy in your marriage. Because his abilities to adapt and adjust will directly affect whether you live happily ever after, or miserably ever after.

3 Steps to Initiating Roles

Since every relationship is different, and there's no cookie-cutter approach to initiating roles in every relationship, customize these steps to fit your relationship.

1. Assess the Scope of the Problem or Task-Oriented Goal

Think before you speak. Shut up! Don't say anything. Keep your thoughts to yourself, for now. When you encounter problems or a task-oriented goal you and your mate need to accomplish, think through the scope of the problem/task-oriented goal by asking yourself these two questions:

1. What's the expected end result or outcome?

2. What's the very next thing that needs to happen in order to resolve/accomplish this?

With question #1, you are identifying what you want the final product or solution to the problem/goal to look like. And with question #2, you are assessing the scope of the problem/goal by trying to figure out all that's involved in solving or accomplishing the problem/goal.

After you answer question #2, ask it again, "What's the very next thing that needs to be done?" Keep asking yourself that question until you have no more answers.

But here's the catch in providing leadership: you don't have to know all the answers to question #2.

Does the president of the United States know all the answers regarding counter-terrorism, US export and import restrictions, or environmental protection policy? Of course not. But he is still responsible for providing leadership to all those areas. And so are you.

All you need to do at this point is to start asking yourself those two questions.

That's one of the responsibilities of a *good* leader—knowing what questions to ask. It demonstrates that you are aware of the direction you want to go. That's all you need to do at this point, just know the expected end result/outcome and ask yourself what's the very next thing that needs to be done to resolve/accomplish it. The answers and details will be fleshed out as you move through the next-steps in the I.C.E.C Leadership Model.

Helpful Hint. Depending on the magnitude of the problem/task-oriented goal, you can choose to make a list of the expected result/outcome and/or the next steps. I usually make list because things get fuzzy after about three next steps.

Learn more about the three steps to initiating roles at www.HisLeadershipHerTrust.com/thebook.

2. Initiate the Roles

Answer this question: *Who's going to do the very next step; and the very next step after that…and so on?*

These are questions you, as the leader, have to answer.

Start off by determining what *you* will do first. Then determine what your mate or others will do. Even if you don't have all the next-steps identified, determine what you will do before you start assigning roles and responsibilities to others.

Take into account your strengths and weaknesses, as well as your mate's. Use past problem solving and task-oriented interactions as a basis to identify each of your strengths and weaknesses, as they should drive which roles and responsibilities each will have. But you *must* identify your role first. This shows that you are being a leader by thinking through what will happen next and initiating roles.

You're not speaking yet. But as you're thinking through this, know that the scope of the problem/ goal you're formulating and the associated roles you are assigning are just preliminary. They are not final. Expect them to change because you haven't taken into account your mate's input, which you will do later.

So even though you've gone through the effort of crafting this plan, you don't provide leadership in a vacuum. You must interact with your mate to establish yourself as a leader. As the group theorists Homans (1950) and Hemphill (1954) discovered, a leader of a group is one who originates the interaction and initiates the roles while solving a mutual problem. So interaction with your mate is a requirement.

And that interaction is not you telling her what you've decided without her input. The interaction you'll eventually have with your mate will lead to determining who will actually perform which roles. But as the leader, you are still responsible for preliminarily assigning the roles.

3.   Initiate the Discussion

Contrary to the title of this subheading, you are still not speaking yet. In this step, you're preparing to speak.

If you've been in a relationship for any length of time, you've likely brought up a topic or started a conversation at the wrong time. And in the middle of the ill-timed conversation, you thought to yourself, "I shouldn't have brought this up right now." Well, this step is meant to avoid that.

Consider the best time to initiate the discussion with your mate. That timing will depend on the problem/goal you're dealing with, and a host of other variables specific to your situation and relationship.

As a guide a) identify a location that allows for the necessary discretion to have the conversation and b) a timeframe that allows sufficient time to have a discussion. You might even want to consider scheduling a time with your mate if your schedules are very busy.

Helpful Hint. I sometimes tell my wife that I want to talk to her about a topic and then I ask her when she is available to talk about it. Given the topic, she knows it's going to either be a short conversation or long one. She then gives me a date and time when we can have this discussion.

Sometimes, you won't be able to pick the location or time to provide leadership. You may happen upon a situation when the problem comes to you and you have to provide leadership ASAP. There's no time to assess the scope of the problem and initiate roles.

In this situation, as a leader, don't panic. Don't freeze like a deer caught in headlights. Don't be combative with the person that has brought the issue to you. And don't find an excuse to leave the room. As a leader, have a predetermined plan for how you will handle situations like this. Have a plan for what to do and say when you don't know what to do or say when you're caught off guard.

You see it in politics all the time. If a reporter asks a candidate a question that he doesn't know or his campaign doesn't want him to answer, they have an aide standing quietly to the side that jumps in and interrupts the press conference and whisks him away to some alleged meeting he's supposedly late for. We've seen it so much that everyone knows what's really going on. The candidate is about to stick his foot in his mouth. But that eject-seat escape plan is his fail-safe tactic that prevents him from saying something that might ruin his candidacy.

Men in relationships need a similar fail-safe tactic. I've seen countless number of men get themselves in trouble by saying something they didn't mean because they were caught off guard. That's how the phrase, "I love you too" is echoed, even though he didn't mean it.

(I'm not the only one that's been caught out there like that...am I?) So in situations like these, have at-the-ready a way to address a range of issues of varying magnitudes that may arise.

Does this require a lot of 'what if' scenario planning? Yes. Do it! So when the "what if" scenario unexpectedly occurs, you will be prepared to provide leadership because you've already initiated the discussion in your mind.

One of my many pre-packaged responses is, "Let me confirm that before I give you an answer and get back to you. I don't want to give you the wrong information." And I usually give them a time or date so they know when to expect my response. That also keeps me accountable to get back to them by that time.

You too should have some pre-packaged responses for how you will handle unexpected problems when they occur. As we move forward, you will learn how to better initiate the discussion under a variety of circumstances.

Helpful Hints:

Practice on the Past

Think through some of the past problems or task-oriented goals you recently resolved and see how you could have assessed the scope, initiated the roles, and initiated the discussion. This will help you to see how to initiate roles in upcoming problems/task-oriented goals.

Think Faster by Thinking Slower

Just like faster internet speeds have the bandwidth to process data more quickly, the faster you can mentally sequence through the three steps for initiating roles, the better leader you will become. You will have the capacity to solve problems faster than you've ever solved them before.

But to think faster, you must first master the way you think through initiating roles. Slowly go through these three steps over and over again until your mind automatically thinks through solving problems in this brand new way.

The more intentionally and slowly you put past and future problems and situations through these three steps of initiating roles, the more quickly you will be able to simultaneously provide leadership in multiple areas because you won't have to think about what to do. You will just be reacting. It will be second nature.

Get bonus content on the three steps to initiating roles at www.HisLeadershipHerTrust.com/thebook.

What's the Very Next Step

The very next step is to communicate and wait. This is the most important chapter of this book. This is when you get to speak. But what you say, or don't say, and how you say it, will be the life or death of your leadership.

For this is where some leaders start to lose it. This is where things begin to become unraveled—when you open your mouth. That's why I wanted to first teach you what to think, so that when you speak, you can tailor your own words and communicate as a leader...as one who wields the craft of leadership like a skilled swordsman.

God-Given Leadership

Unbeknownst to me, I didn't know how sensitive and emotional my wife was until after we got married. I, on the other hand, was on the opposite side of the sensitive and emotional spectrum. I wouldn't say I was insensitive. More so, I was indifferent. I could masterfully separate my emotions from my behavior. I could like you, but act like I didn't. Or, I couldn't stand you, but act like I liked you. This skill was cultivated during my tomfoolery and hijinks days. And I took pride in this skill set.

So...when I got married, I initially didn't know how handle the flood of varying emotions I experienced throughout the day. But what I quickly learned was, since I could control my behavior by separating them from my emotions, I could better control my responses to her emotional high and low tides. Plus, I added the skill of gauging her emotions by asking pointed questions to find out what kind of mood she was in. Since there always seemed to be some wave of emotion coming ashore, I learned to be like a duck. However high or low her tide of emotions ebbed, like a duck, I'd rise or lower with her tide. I perfected how to counterbalance and stabilize the emotional undercurrent in our household.

In my experience, husbands go wrong when they tried to control the emotional tide rather than adjusting to it. Emotions are a response to a unique set of events. So I didn't try to control them. I took on the responsibility trying to control the set of events that create the emotions.

Once I figured out what set of events affect which emotions, I'd adjust my behavior accordingly, regardless of how I was feeling. If Bernie was in a really happy mood, then I'd be really excited when engaging with her, even if I could care less about what she was happy about. If she was really down, I'd be really engaged to find out why she was unhappy and try to fix it...if possible.

Don't get me wrong. I wasn't running around the house on pins and needles, bracing myself for the next emotional tsunami. No sir! What I was, am, and will always be, is a very purposeful husband who is deliberate about deriving the optimal peace in my marriage, while still accomplishing the goals we established for our household. And I do it with the understanding that because my wife is not like me, I am willing to make allowances for her different ways and preferences for how things get done. This is what I tried to explain to Bernie that night in the kitchen. Our roles in the marriage were different. Her roles were important and more tangible. My roles were just as important and more intangible. And the recognition of both roles needed to be respected.

It took more arguing that night to convince her that I actually was doing something. And as we continued into months three and four, she started to notice how pliable I was, able to adjust to counterbalance her emotions so that the Wiggins Household would achieve its day to day goals and its long term goal to create a happy peaceful home, even at the expense of my own preferences. What I later came to realize was I was simply providing leadership in my family.

Chapter 6:

Step 2: Communicate—
The Process of Influence

Communicate Your Task-Oriented Goal First

In my freshman year of college, I took Communications 101. Now, I didn't know I needed to know learn to communicate because I had been communicating just fine up until that point. But in that class, I learned that there is a standard communication process, which includes a sender, a message, and a receiver.

That's the basics. But the question you need answered is, "How do I communicate as a leader in my relationship?" For starters, as discussed in the previous chapter, you first have to initiate the roles.

Your very next step is to communicate the goal or expected outcome to your mate. Even if you don't fully know how you're going to accomplish it yet, a leader first communicates what he wants his end goal to be. This establishes the task-oriented goal before it becomes the common goal. Because at this point, it's just your goal. You don't have her buy-in yet.

Next, communicate the details on how you want to accomplish this goal. Welcome her input to obtain buy-in. Once she buys-in, it becomes a common goal. Now you can begin the process of influencing the movement of your group toward that common goal.

The Process of influence

"But how do I do that?" That's the big question. Providing leadership to go shopping this weekend is rather simple. But how do I provide leadership on some more difficult problems or task-oriented goals?

Those are the questions I asked myself when we were about six years into my marriage. We just paid off a lot of debt. We moved to a new neighborhood. My career was on an upward swing. I had position and status in leadership at church. All was well. Except I felt like we weren't *doing* anything. We would vacation over here, eat out over there, and hang out with friends and family. I felt like we were zombies, walking around just *living*, but with no purposeful intent. I knew I needed to lead us out of this passive existence.

But I didn't have a clue where to go or how to leads us there. The leadership skills I had in the beginning of my marriage had run its course. I needed to learn how to be a better leader. So, in 2005, 13 years after graduating from undergrad, I went back to school to earn a master's in organizational leadership.

After graduating in 2006, I continued reading all these different books and articles about leadership. I understood what leadership is, but what specifically do I do? How do I translate this into being a better husband?

Do I just start barking orders, 'You do this. I'mma do that,' like "My Way" Man? Do I try to bribe her? "If you do this, then I'll buy you that." That's not sustainable. I'll go broke trying to influence her to help me paint each wall in the living room. What if I speak in a soft and caring voice? Caring, yes, but soft? NO! If a caring voice is the answer, is that going to be my new process for influencing? That can't be it. What's a brother to do?

These questions sparked my quest to find out what the heck the process of influence is. What I ultimately discovered was so enlightening, it revolutionized the way I think, how I speak, what I say, and when I say it. It gave me the tools I needed to say and do the right thing at the right time as a leader in my marriage. And learning the process of influence and using it in your relationship will help you do the same thing too.

Three Characteristics of Influence

You need to know and understand these characteristics because, contrary to what you may have heard, influence is not leadership:

1) **Influence exists both within a group and organizationally structured relationship.** Unlike the requirement for leadership where there must be a common goal for leadership to exist, influence does not require a common goal. Influence can be completely for selfish personal gains or for mutual common benefit.

2) **The process of influencing contains multiple steps.** It's not a one-time event where you do step one and you have successfully influenced someone.

3) The process of influence lasts throughout the completion of the common goal. It is not something where you complete the multiple steps at the beginning and then you're done. The process of influencing starts in the beginning and doesn't end until after you've accomplished the common goal.

The Process of Influence

The process of influencing is made up of two components: power and persuasion. The process of influencing is *the use of power to persuade*.

Now here's where it gets interesting. If you understand the concept of power and how to use it to persuade, then you will know exactly how to provide leadership within an organizationally structured relationship.

So let's first start with understanding what power is. Then we'll discuss how to use it to persuade.

Chapter 7:
Power

The topic of power may seem scary to some because it may seem like I'm promoting men to be controlling, abusive, or heavy-handed in their leadership. Admittedly, when I first came to understand what power is, I had a hard time imagining myself in a room full of couples and telling men to use their power to influence their relationship. I could physically feel the eye-daggers piercing my flesh from the women in the room, let alone the abandonment I'd feel from the men who would instantly side with their mate out of self-preservation.

Let's face it, there are plenty of negative connotations associated with "power," with axioms like "abuse of power," "power hungry," or "power grab." These attributes of power were detailed in the writings of Niccolo Machiavelli in his 1513 book, *The Prince*, where he encouraged the use of deceit, coercion, deviousness, and any other means necessary to maintain power.[21]

---

[21] (Bass, 2008)

All of these forms of power generate feelings of discomfort, unease, and overall disgust. But these negative connotations of power all refer to how power is *used*. They do not define what power *is*.

There are also some positive connotations of power, such as powerful, empowered, source of power, and the like. These words convey a sense of strength and might. But they too are nondescript.

Influence and leadership are inextricably tied to power. It is absolutely impossible to influence a group or provide leadership without it. Therefore, you must understand what power is and how it is used. Then you'll know how to properly use it to persuade and provide leadership in your relationship.

What is Power?

Since the 1930s, psychologists and behavior and organizational scientists have thoroughly researched power in politics, manager/subordinate relationships, personal relationships, and many other areas. French and Raven's[22] landmark discovery identified five uses of power: Expert

---

[22] French and Raven (1959)

Power, Referent Power, Reward Power, Coercive Power, and Legitimate Power. But the best definition of power is a compilation of the decades of research.

Power is the *control over the access to or distribution of resources.*

The first and last words in this definition, *control* and *resources*, are the first and last things I want you to know about power. Power is the control of resources, not people.

Power Resources

There are six power resources: **t**ime, **m**aterial **r**esources, **i**nformation, **p**unishments, **a**ffection, and **r**ewards. To remember all of them, use the acronym T.R.I.P.A.R. (pronounced TRIPPER).

Let's look at each power resource individually:

Time

One who controls the access to and distribution of your time possesses a degree of power (e.g., I control how much quality time I choose to give to my wife on the weekends.)

Likewise, if you control the access to and distribution of someone else's time, you possess a degree of power (e.g., If I'm out shopping with my wife, she has control over how much of my time will be spent shopping.)

Material Resources

Material resources are anything tangible or physical (e.g., you allow your wife to use your car while hers is in the shop.)

Financial resources include money, assets, property, stock, bonds, or commodities (e.g., If my wife makes more money than me, then she has access to more of the financial resources than I do.) Power also extends to the authority to grant access to funds or the authority to distribute funds (e.g., banks and mortgage lending institutions). Credit is also a financial resource—both the credit card limit and your credit score. If my wife has a credit score of 800, she has a significantly higher degree of power than if she had a credit score of 600.

Human resources refers to the use of people to accomplish a task. If my wife asks me to do some handyman project around the house, I control whether I choose to distribute my human resources to that effort.

Human resources also includes the authority you have over someone else's human resources (e.g., you give your wife permission to start a home-based business). Lastly, human resources include a unique physical ability, like a strong man able to lift a heavy piece of furniture.

Information

Information can be knowledge, understanding, or wisdom that you possess. It can also be something like knowing directions to a restaurant, or knowing specific information about how to set up a home computer network. I have a degree of power based on how much of my information I choose to grant one access to or how much I choose to distribute.

Punishment

When a child acts up in school, his parents punish him by taking away some privileges. That is the most common form of punishment you're probably familiar with because we've all been on one side or the other of this equation.

But punishment is more than withholding something. It's also giving something that is unwanted. For example, if I forget to do something my wife is counting on me to do, then she'll give me major attitude, a million questions about why I didn't do it, and this look of disapproval that I can't stand.

Affect

The term "affect" is a psychological term that refers to any feeling or emotion a person may have. Whereas *affection* is understood to convey a positive feeling, *affect* is a non-specific feeling that can be either positive or negative. For example, "The *affect* I have for you varies from day to day." So, for the purpose of understanding power resources, I will refer to feelings under the broader category of *affect*.

With that said, you have the ability to control the access to and distribution of your own affect, and the affects of others. For example, I controlled my distribution of positive affect by deciding when I will tell my wife how much I appreciate her. Conversely, I could say something that's offensive that would make her angry. This isn't recommended. But I wanted to make the point that you do possess a degree of power if you can control the distribution of another person's affect, negatively or positively.

Rewards

Whereas punishment is withholding something that is wanted and distributing something that is unwanted, rewards are the opposite. A reward is distributing something that is wanted, and withholding something that is unwanted…like being released from punishment earlier that originally stated.

When I was 15, I wanted to get my driver's license when I turned 16. My uncle Gerald told me, "If you make the honor roll, then I'll give you my old car." Once I heard that, it was on! I was determined to bang out that fourth marking period and make the honor roll so I could get my own set of wheels.

In my uncle's case, he controlled the access to and distribution of something I wanted, which I considered a reward for making the honor roll.

When the school year ended, I couldn't wait to get my report card. And for the first time in high school, I made the honor roll—a 3.0. That was a marked improvement for a solid C student. And true to his word, Uncle G drove up from North Carolina to Maryland and brought his 1981 5-

speed stick shift Toyota Corolla Tercel (that's when the Corolla and the Tercel was one car). I named it Kevin.

It's important for you to know power is not control over a person. In fact, the only time someone has power over you is when you give it to them.

The Use of Power

As you can see, power is neither negative nor positive. It's neither good nor bad. It's neither male nor female dominant.

So I reject the notion that power is a heavy-handed, abusive show of force. At a very basic level, power is just the resources you've acquired over time (i.e., financial, material resources, and informational).

But…*how* you control those resources is what people generally see and equate to power.

You probably wouldn't look at what Uncle G did as a negative use of power. You wouldn't accuse him of abusing his power by controlling his access to and distribution of his car in order to manipulate me into getting good grades. It's fair to say that he used his power to influence me to get good grades.

See, it's the *use* of power that determines whether it was used for positive or negative purposes.

Power is About You

The use of power is not necessarily about what you have, but it's more about who you are. In other words, it's about how you control the resources you've acquired.

The power resource of *time*, for example, is given equally to everyone. Everyone has the same 24 hours in a day. Sixty minutes in an hour. Control over your time is actually determined by you. As an adult, you have 100 percent control over your time—that is, until you give up control to something else, like your job, the military, or church.

You usually give up control of your time for money. For example, you've agreed to give up control of eight hours of your day to your job in exchange for a specific dollar amount per hour.

However, you could negotiate your time for something else, like giving it to a church or a social organization. In those cases, you're not negotiating for money. It is likely for some other philanthropic reason.

In either case, once you give up control of your time, you have now decreased your degree of power over your own power resource. Wherein you had 100 percent control over your own time, you now have 66 percent degree of control over the access to and distribution of the power resource of time (24 hours–8 hours = 16 hours or 66 percent of remaining hours in a day).

Granted, you are being compensated for those eight hours with money—a financial power resource. But in exchange, you've given up 33 percent of the access and distribution of your own time and handed it over to your boss. Now, he or she has a degree of power over your time.

Take the power resource of *information*. You control 100 percent of the access to and distribution of your information—that is, until you decide sell the information to become a computer consultant, tax preparer, or a musician. Once you did that, the person who hired you has a degree of power over the access of your information.

Conversely, in the instance of the musician, the better musician you are, the more control you have over how much it costs for someone to access your musical mastery. If you're really good, you can charge top dollar for someone to hire you as a musician. But if you're unknown and just trying to make it in the business, you'll play for free outside a music studio, like Justin Bieber did, just for the opportunity for someone to access your information power resource.

How Do You Acquire Power Resources?

Your Past Experiences Define Your Truth and Reality
At a very basic level, power is a combination of all the professional expertise, heartbreak, relationships, financial assets, education, life lessons, and overall wisdom you've accumulated from your entire life's experiences.

All these life experiences have not only created your power resources, they also created your value system. Your value system is derived from various sources, but primarily originates from your family.

Whatever your upbringing, your family has a big influence on who you are today. What you experienced from childhood to adulthood has shaped what you believe is true or false, right or wrong, good or bad, etc.

If your parents, for example, made you turn off the TV and the lights and go to the basement or sit on the floor in the living room during a bad thunderstorm, it's highly likely you'll do the same thing as an adult. Why? Because your *reality* and *truth* was that thunderstorms are to be respected and revered in silence.

But if the family who lived next door to you sat on the porch and watch the beauty of the storm roll pass, their *reality* and *truth* was that thunderstorms were wondrously beautiful in all its fury and were to be witnessed and admired up close.

Your Past Experiences Create Your Belief and Value Systems

From the same thunderstorm, there are two completely different perspectives of what is real and true. These beliefs shape what we believe in the world to be right or wrong, good or bad, acceptable or unacceptable, worthy or unworthy.

But you just don't get your beliefs from your family. Your race and the era in which you grew up also helped define how you look at the world. Black families that lived in the South during the civil rights movement of the '60s and '70s have a much different perspective of what is real and true than white families that lived in the Northwest region during the same time. And the children of those families that went to college, moved away, or found a job in a different state during the 80s and 90s, have a completely different perspective about what is real and true than their parents did at the same age. From the baby boomers to Generation Y, race and age have a huge influence on what you believe.

The geographic region you were raised in also significantly impacts who you are. In political campaigns, we often hear candidates tout their good Midwestern values. Or maybe you're familiar with someone who has prepared for you some good ole Southern home cooking.

And of course, your religion has a set of beliefs and behaviors that are predetermined. How strongly you hold fast to them influences your belief of what is good or bad, right or wrong, acceptable or unacceptable behavior.

All these different life-factors create a set of beliefs for what you perceive as right or wrong. For whatever reason, you've found their truths and applications valuable and worth having in your life for your survival and/or happiness.

Each one of those beliefs is its own *value*. These values cover every area of your life: personal, sociological, demographical, regional, religious, financial, professional, sexual, etc. You started collecting these values as a child and you never stopped.

And the integration of all your different values is what makes up your value system.

Your Experiences Create Your Power Resources

From childhood to adulthood, your interactions in school, relationships, work, church, etc., all gave you a wealth of experiences to draw from. Through the years, as you interacted with people and society, the values you acquired were either reaffirmed, or disproved and replaced with more acceptable values of what you now believe is right and wrong. And based on this evolving value system, you've navigated your life in pursuit of the things you thought best for your survival and happiness.

For example, some people valued going to college after high school and some valued immediately entering the workforce. Some people valued a career making a lot of money, while some valued pursing a patriotic service in the military. Neither is right nor wrong. It's all a matter of what your value system permits you to pursue.

Your value system has driven you to navigate your life in pursuit of those things you value. And it's the variety of things you've acquired in your pursuits, and how you acquired them is what created your power resources, your TRIPAR, which are valuable to you and other people.

Danny is a college student who valued going to college right after high school. He's a valuable resource to a company that wants to hire a college graduate for an entry-level position.

Kim valued entering the workforce immediately after high school. She has gained four years of work experience during the same time Danny was in college. Those four years of experience are a valuable resource to a company looking to hire someone with four-plus years of experience to be the manager of their new store.

Each person, through their value system and life experiences, possesses power resources of information and time. Their power resources are both sought after by two different companies. But Danny and Kim control 100 percent of the access to and distribution of their time and information.

It was their value systems that prompted each of them to pursue the path they felt was right, acceptable, and valuable for their life. How much those companies desire the power resources they've acquired will determine how much financial resources (money) they're willing to pay to obtain them.

Power Struggles in Relationships

This is a basically how power is used. Two or more parties enter into a negotiation where multiple power resources are being exchanged. A power struggle ensues. And each uses their full arsenal of TRIPAR as leverage to get what they want. Those who are more skilled at knowing which power resources to use and how to use them, are more successful at getting what they want.

In an organizationally structured relationship, there are power struggles for control over the access to and distribution of the power resources within the relationship. Depending on one's value system governing certain resources, the balance of power will shift back and forth.

For example, a man tries to provide leadership when trying to solve a problem about money. But he is met with stanch resistance from his mate. Eventually, he yields to her preference. Why? Because his value system permitted him to do so.

Compare him to the horrible leader, "My Way" Man. His value system permits him to put up a blistering fight, intent on wearing his mate down until she gives in. His value system permits him to get his way, regardless of merit.

How Will You Use Your Power?

As a leader, how will you use your power? Will your use of power support its negative or positive connotations? The real answer is it depends on the totality of your life experiences, which created your value system, which dictate how you'll use power to control the TRIPAR in your relationship.

If your life experiences required you to be combative, assertive, and aggressive in order to get what you want, then you've found that approach valuable, acceptable, and beneficial to have in your life for your survival and/or happiness. That is likely how you will use power to control the TRIPAR in your relationship.

On the other hand, if your life experiences called for you to be passive, unassertive, and you let people have their way because you've found avoiding conflict valuable for your survival and/or happiness, you will likely adopt that same approach when using TRIPAR in your relationship to solve problems.

Learn how to acquire power and use it properly. Get bonus content at www.HisLeadershipHerTrust.com/thebook.

Danny and Kim Pt. 1: The Meeting

Let's look at this example of how a couple, Danny and Kim, used power to control the resources within their relationship to resolve a very common problem that arises in every relationship— money. As the story is told, Danny and Kim met when Danny was out shopping for some suits for his new job. Kim was out shopping with her mother and two sisters. As Kim walked into the store, she saw Danny coming out a dressing room, trying on a suit. She noted to herself that he looked nice in the suit as she sifted through the racks in the store.

Danny picked three suits. But he was only going to buy two. He couldn't decide which two to buy. So Danny gathered all three suits and headed to the cashier. His plan was to make a decision at the cashier. As he stood there perplexed and struggling, Kim happened to be walking by.

"Excuse me! Which suit should I put back, this one or that one? I can't make up my mind," Danny asked Kim.

Startled by the abruptness of the question, Kim paused. She took a look at Danny, then at the suits. "Well, this one I saw you trying on when you came out the dressing room, and it looked nice. So I say keep that one," she replied.

"Done!" He turned to the cashier and tells her to ring up the suit Kim picked out. Then he turned back to Kim. "So you think I look nice?" he said jokingly with devilish smile.

"I didn't say that," she tried to say with an attitude while fighting back an emerging smile. "I said the suit looked nice on you." she retorted as she rolled her eyes.

"I don't know, maybe it's me, but that still sounds like you're still saying I look nice. I don't know." He turned and asked the cashier, "What do you think?"

The cashier smiled but shook her head as if to say, "I'm not in this." Danny turned back to Kim. But Kim, now embarrassed, is looking for a gracious exit.

"Whatever!" Kim said as she rolls her eyes again and slowly turned to walk away. "Goodbye. Enjoy your suit."

"Stop!" Danny commands. "Don't you take another step!" he says in a slow quiet stern voice.

Kim's eyes got wide. The cashier's eyes got wide too. Kim slowly turned with an attitude like, "What did you just say?"

The cashier is frozen. "How you gonna just walk right out the store without a proper introduction? Stay right there. Let me finish up this transaction so I can do a proper introduction. Then you can be on your way."

Danny turned to the cashier and loudly whispered so Kim could hear him, "Now I need you to hurry up. Because if she leaves this store before you finish this transaction, then I'm going to return these suits and complain to your manager that you're a horribly slow cashier. Feel me?"

The cashier laughed and quickly proceeded to ring up Danny's suits.

When he turned to the cashier, in so doing, he turned his back to Kim. So he couldn't see if she was still standing there or was leaving the store. He was really testing her to see if she'd stay or go.

This was a challenge for Kim. She was torn. She wanted to walk away just out of spite—because Danny told her not to move. But she also wanted to give Danny a chance to introduce himself. So she did what any self-respecting woman would do. She walked away, slowly. But she didn't leave the store. She started looking at clothes on the racks around the cashier. This way she could save face by not standing there waiting for Danny. But she still allowed Danny time to finish the transaction, find her, and introduce himself.

The cashier finally finished the transaction. Danny gathered his clothes and turned around. He saw Kim three racks away looking at clothes. But she had her back to him. He walked over to her. As he approached, he opened his mouth to say something clever. Without looking up and with much attitude, Kim jumped in: "I don't know *who* you think you are, ordering me to stand still! You musta lost…"

"I'm Daniel," he interrupted, giving her a warm charming smile as he extends his hand. "But my friends call me Danny. I'm the one that couldn't let you leave the store without first thanking you for helping me pick out this suit. I'm the one who couldn't let you leave the store without knowing your name or without some way of contacting you again. And I'm the nice looking one that wanted to tell you that I think you look nice too."

Kim was stuck. She kept her head down as she continued rummaging through the clothes. She didn't want him to see her blushing. Kim quickly collected herself, looked up, briefly made eye contact and shook his hand. "I'm Kim," she said, trying not to smile but failing miserably.

Danny and Kim exchanged numbers and start dating several months later. They dated for five years before they eventually got married. When we meet up with Danny and Kim next, they've been married for three years.

Danny and Kim Pt. 2: The Anniversary Discussion

The Use of Power Within a Relationship When Solving a Problem

It's been a tight few months in Danny and Kim's household, financially speaking. They've just had some unexpected expenses over the past few months. A $50 oil change turned into an unexpected $1,000 repair. Combine that with a pesky $100 speeding camera ticket. Plus a larger than normal monthly grocery bill because Danny's family visited for a week a month ago.

While going over the monthly bills, Danny remembers that they need to start setting some money aside for their anniversary trip in three months. After all, he doesn't want to go on their anniversary with the bare minimum. He wants to vacation baller-style. So Danny picks a best time to discuss this with Kim.

Danny and Kim sit down at the kitchen table one evening as he presents his idea. Based on Danny's value system, he wants to pay the minimum amount on the bills and put some money into savings for the next three months. Then continue aggressively paying off their bills after their trip.

Kim disagrees. Based on her value system, she wants to use whatever extra money they have to pay off their debt as soon as possible and then save for the anniversary trip. She's even willing to decrease the amount of money they spend on their trip in order to pay off their debts before they leave. Kim just can't see going on an expensive vacation while they have outstanding bills waiting for them when they get back home.

Their discussion started out amenable. Everyone was cool tempered. Danny and Kim pleasantly exchanged advantages and disadvantages of their respective sides. They both made valid points for their own position. But neither was giving way.

After a while, Kim started getting a little irritated. Irritation turned into frustration. She was getting heated. Her tone and non-verbals teetered on the edge of taking the conversation into a full-blown argument. But before it went too far, Danny decided to shut it down and yielded to Kim's preference.

After the discussion, Kim left the kitchen table happy and content that they decided to go with her approach. However, Danny was not happy about it.

Before you rush into the "If I was Danny, I woulda..." let's examine what happened in this frequently occurring problem that arises in relationships. First, there was a problem to solve. Danny identified it. He did the right thing to provide leadership to the situation by initiating roles. He assessed the scope of the problem and came up with a solution, instead of ignoring the problem and leaving up to his wife to come up with a solution. He initiated the discussion by picking the best time to discuss it with Kim. Then he communicated his plan for how to solve the problem and waited for feedback. These are all the hallmarks for providing leadership.

Danny started out well. But what happened? Did he maintain it? Did he fall prey to the Adam syndrome and let Kim take over? Why didn't he stand his ground and insist on his way? After all, he was the one who initiated the discussion.

The answer to these questions all boils down to what Danny's life experiences and value system determined to be right, valuable, and beneficial to his life. And Danny used his power differently than you would have expected.

During their discussion, Kim didn't like Danny's proposal. Based on her value system, she felt very strongly about how and where the financial resources should be distributed.

But so did Danny. His value system just as strongly impressed upon him how and where the financial resources should be allocated. But the distribution of financial resources was not the only power resource at play in this discussion. See, Kim's value system permitted her to introduce another power resource into the negotiation to help her control the distribution of those financial resources: *affect*. Without any discomfort or guilt, she was willing to introduce negative *affect* and ratchet up the conversation into a full-blown argument, in order to control the distribution of financial resources.

But Danny wasn't no punk in this exchange. He didn't just crumble, back down, or sit passively while Kim's fury raged. Actually, it was Danny that controlled the outcome of their decision.

See, according to Danny's value system, he placed a high value on a peaceful relationship, void of drama and nonsense. He had limits on how much negative *affect* he would allow in a conversation about money for this vacation. So instead of letting their peaceful conversation turn into an argument, causing their anniversary to be about how much money they're spending and not about their relationship, he controlled Kim's distribution of her negative *affect* by yielding to her preference.

Now I know some guys might be thinking, *all Kim has to do to get her way is start an argument and Danny will back down.* No, although for some men, this might be the case. But for this particular issue, Danny valued peace over the power. Danny could have very well escalated the argument with Kim. He could have come back even harder and more forceful and argued her down until she gave in to his "My Way" Man style.

Instead, he decided not to. And it wasn't because he didn't have it in him to fight for his position. On the contrary, it was his values system that allowed him to yield to Kim's preference and maintain control over the peaceful *affect* he valued and enjoyed in their relationship. It's the classic "pick your battles" strategy.

Danny showed a great use of power and leadership. He was willing to take the "L" on a singular issue for the sake of the peace and tranquility in their entire relationship. Money comes and goes, but a peaceful household, money cannot buy.

From one perspective, it seems like Kim has the power in their relationship. She controls the distribution of their financial resources by adding negative *affect* to the discussion. But was Kim wrong? Did she use her power to support the negative connotations? That depends on your value system.

For Kim, her values are based on what she believes is right and wrong about money. From her experiences from childhood to adulthood, it is perfectly acceptable to ratchet up the level of negative emotional *affect* to fight for what she thinks is right. In fact, in her eyes, to not do so is considered wrong and unacceptable.

Conversely, Danny holds different values concerning money. Based on what he believes is right and wrong, it is unnecessary and sometimes unacceptable to fight over money to the degree that it disrupts the positive atmosphere in their relationship. After all, he reconciles, it's only money. And the peace within their relationship is more important than how or where this money is distributed.

So was Kim wrong? Not according to Kim's value system.

Was Danny wrong? Not according to Danny's values system.

These differences in values are why a couple can look at the same problem and see two different ways of solving it. And neither approach makes sense to the other. These differences are the source of much frustration and misunderstanding.

Couples who don't see eye to eye on how to solve a problem or accomplish a task-oriented goal struggle because they don't understand their mate's value system.

And without that understanding, they can't find the logic in your mate's decision-making. "She's crazy." "He's stupid."

The couple that makes an effort to understand and accept their mate's value system, even if you don't like it or agree with it, will be able to solve problems and accomplish task-oriented goals much more fluidly and efficiently than those who don't have such understanding.

Desire and Dependence Determines How Much Power You Have

Danny and Kim's problem-solving episode reveals the key to how power is created, gained, and lost. Power is created by someone's desire for, or dependence on, TRIPAR. Power is gained and lost based on how much someone has a desire for, or dependence on, the TRIPAR you control. The greater desire or dependence someone has for the TRIPAR you control, the more power you have (figure 1).

But you're not the only one with power. Conversely, the amount of power someone else has is based on how much you have a desire for, or are dependent on, the TRIPAR they control. Thus, the greater desire or dependence you have for the TRIPAR someone else controls, the less power you have (figure 2).

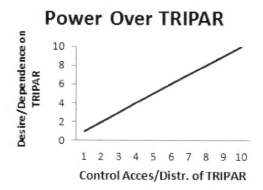

Figure 1

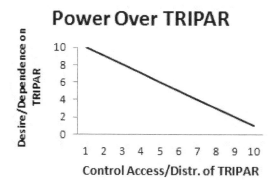

Figure 2

High Desire and Low Control = A Low Degree of Power

Let's look at Danny and Kim's situation. From Danny's perspective, he was the one that came up with the idea of saving money instead of paying off bills. He was also the one who regularly handled the bills. He generally determined who was going to get paid how much and when. So Danny had a high degree of control over the financial resources in their household. And Kim had little control over the finances and pretty much went along with (dependency) what Danny decided. On a scale of 1-10, let's say Danny's power over the finances was a 9 and Kim's was a 2 (figure 3).

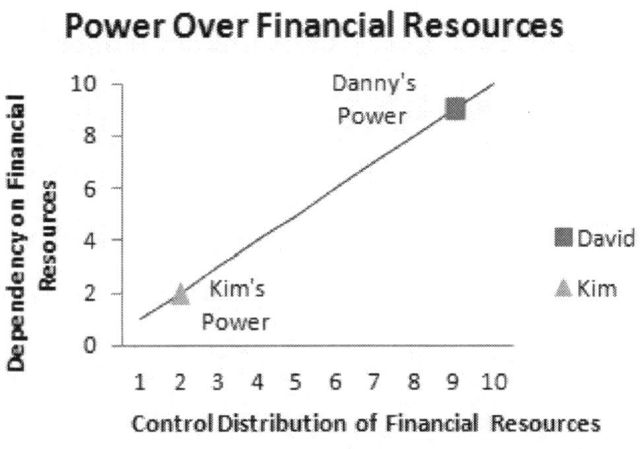

Figure 3

Now, Kim didn't like the idea of putting money aside for the anniversary trip off the bat. Kim was depending on those financial resources to pay off bills, not to spend it frivolously while on their anniversary. The more they talked about it, the less and less she liked it. So much so that she injected negative *affect* to try to control how the money would be spent.

As Kim's interest in controlling the distribution of those resources increased, so did her power over those resources—to a 10. The power struggle is now on.

With Kim ratcheting up her vibrato to control how the money would be spent, the tension between the two started to increase. And Danny's interest or dependency in controlling those resources started to decrease. As you know, he ultimately gave up his control over how those resources would be spent, thus decreasing his power down to a 4 (figure 4).

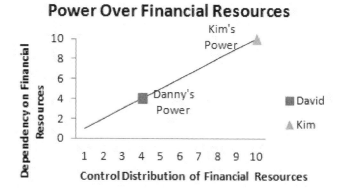

Figure 4

NOTICE: If Danny would have desired to keep his desire to control the financial resources up to a 10, a huge fight would have broken out. That is the quintessential power struggle. The loser would have been the one who felt it wasn't worth it and decreased their desire to control the money. This kind of power struggle happens in relationships all the time, and usually it's the relationship that loses.

How You Use Power Makes Power Good or Bad

Did Kim use her power to support the negative or positive connotations of power? Well, it depends. Some may applaud Kim's assertiveness. Others might feel she needs to be more willing to compromise than to take it to 10 when she doesn't get her way.

Whether you feel Kim's approach was a positive or negative use of power totally depends on your value system. Contrary to what most people think about so-called "family values," every family's value system is different. Some people seek equitable outcomes. Some people seek outcomes skewed to their advantage. Some people, like Danny, seek peace instead of preference. Some people, like Kim, seek, preference over peace. It all depends on your experiences and what you've found to be good or bad, right or wrong, etc. for your survival and/or happiness.

And the aggregate of those experiences determines how you use power. For power is ultimately not what you have, but who you are.

Using Power in Relationships

As you move forward in your relationship with your mate, know that power exists in a relationship to solve problems and accomplish goals. As the case with Danny and Kim, power was only used when there was a problem to solve.

The signs of good influence and leadership is when you, the man, use your power to control the resources within the relationship—both yours and hers—to solve problems or accomplish goals.

But Christ-like leadership is when you use your power to control the resources in order to solve problems and accomplish goals in service to other people.

With the entire arsenal of heavenly power at his disposal, Jesus used his power for the benefit of others, even in death. With his power resources, he controlled the distribution of *punishment* by accepting the punishment of death that God required for Adam's sin and everyone else's sin thereafter.

And He controlled the access to *rewards*, by allowing anyone who wanted to be reunited with God to receive salvation. Jesus said, to those who believe in me, you can have access to the Kingdom of God.

A Power Warning

Avoid using power in *every* part of your relationship. This will turn your relationship into a constant power struggle, full of negotiating and bartering. That is a misuse of power in a relationship. As I stated earlier, you don't need a common goal to influence someone. You just need to know how to control the TRIPAR while solving a problem or pursuing a goal, and the value system to justify doing whatever it takes to tip the scales in your favor.

In relationships, controlling the *affect* for selfish gain is most egregious and widely prevalent. In some instances, if a man doesn't get his way, he will withdraw from interaction with his mate and disconnect emotionally as a form of punishment. Conversely, we've all heard of or experienced women who withhold intimacy or sex from their mate as a form of punishment in order to get their way.

These examples are an abuse of power. They reinforce negative connotations of power. From a leadership standpoint, these abuses display a distorted use of your power that is enabled by your value system.

You should not be using your power to advance your own selfish agenda. This bad practice creates a bad precedent for how to solve problems in your relationship. It will spread to all areas of your relationship.

Your relationship will transform into a constant struggle for power and tit-for-tat bickering. You'll end up negotiating for common courtesies. And bartering for affection in exchange for material possessions will be a common practice. The purpose of power in relationships is to marshal all the available power resources to achieve the common goal—not your own self-interest.

Using Power to Solve Problems or Accomplish Task-Oriented Goals

Leaders Communicate Persuasively

The process of influence is the use of power to persuade. If power is about which power resources you've accumulated, then persuasion is about how you use those power resources to influence your mate toward accomplishing a common goal.

If power is created by your personal experiences and value system, then persuasion is about how your value system permits you to use the wisdom gained from your experiences.

If power is not about what you have, but about who you are, then persuasion is about the confidence you have in who you are and how to use that confidence to influence others.

Chapter 8:

Persuasion

Danny and Kim Pt 3: The Return Home

With Danny and Kim's new financial agreement in place, they were able to pay off the bills Kim wanted and save some extra money for their anniversary trip. But not as much as Danny wanted. He wasn't mad though. Kim let Danny spend a majority of their money on the activities and items he wanted to buy. So Danny felt the trade-off was worth it.

Danny and Kim return home. Danny takes their bags upstairs to their bedroom and starts to unpack. Kim remains downstairs in the kitchen and sorts through the week's worth of mail and checks the voicemail. She picks up the phone and puts in the passcode. She yells upstairs, "Danny, do you want to listen to the messages?"

"No. Just let me know if there's anything worth listening to.

Kim puts the phone on speaker so she can sort through the mail and check the messages at the same time. There are 11 messages. Most of them are solicitations. Halfway through the messages, she abruptly stops sorting through the mail. She presses one on the phone to replay the message.

"Danny! Come here!" she yells in a firm voice.

"What is it?" he yells back inquisitively.

"You've gotta listen to this message."

"Just tell me what it says."

"*Come here!*"

Sensing the seriousness of her tone, Danny drops what he's doing and heads downstairs, not knowing what to expect. But based on Kim's tone, he puts on his game face. He braces himself for some news that he figures will inevitably shift his mood from vacation mode back to real-life mode.

As he reaches the bottom step and walks over to Kim, he doesn't say a word. He just has this intense look on his face, like "This better be real good." Kim responds to his silent stare with a wide-eyed stare of her own. "OMG, are you ready for this?" her face seems to say. As Danny reaches the kitchen counter where she's standing, their eyes are still locked on each other. Nobody's saying a word.

There's a quiet intensity in the room that cements the transition back to real life. Kim breaks eye contact to look down at the phone. She puts her thumb on the number 1 button. Just before she presses it, she looks back up at Danny and says, "Welcome home." *beep*

Persuasion

When couples try to solve a problem or accomplish a task-oriented goal, it involves controlling the TRIPAR of the relationship in one direction or the other—as we saw with Danny and Kim. Sometimes, the couple agrees how TRIPAR will be used, but sometimes they don't. And when they don't agree and a decision has to be made one way or the other, that's when the tool of persuasion kicks in.

Persuasion is the attempt to change someone's beliefs, affect (feelings or emotions), intentions, or behavior.[23] To make it easier to remember these attributes, I use the acronym BAIB, pronounced "babe."

---

[23] Jaccard, 1981

Researchers have long studied various persuasive theories and methods. The most popular one was done by Yale University's communication program in 1953 under the direction of Carl Hovland.[24] This research project laid the foundation for how persuasion is used in every area of society—from supervisor-subordinate communications, to sales and advertising campaigns, to the facial expression politicians should not make during a debate.

Understanding someone's BAIB is key to successfully persuading your mate. I'm not talking about tricking her or duping her into believing a lie. I'm talking about knowing what to say, when to say it, and how to say it in order to successfully persuade her to solve a problem and accomplish your common goals.

Hierarchy of Persuasion Attributes

Persuasive attributes have a hierarchy. Depending on the problem you're solving or the task-oriented goal you're trying to accomplish, you may need to change one or more of these four attributes. The most difficult attribute to change is one's beliefs and the easiest is one's behavior.

---

[24] Hovland, Janis, and Kelley, 1953

Belief

The most difficult attribute to change is your mate's belief because her beliefs are based on her value system, which is based on a lifetime of experiences that she believes is right, good, acceptable, and necessary for her survival and/or happiness. To change her beliefs, you have to mount a significant enough argument against her lifetime of experience to convince her to abandon her beliefs and accept yours.

In Danny and Kim's original issue about control over how the money would be distributed, Danny unsuccessfully tried to persuade Kim to save more money for the trip by trying to change her *intention* to pay off bills first. He failed because he only tried to persuade her to change one attribute—her *intentions*. He also needed to change her *belief*.

Based on Kim's value system growing up, she *believed* that being in debt was bad. You pay your bills first, put money aside for savings, and then you can spend what's left over on discretionary items. Because of this *belief*, she always *intended* on paying off bills first, even though Danny was the one responsible for handling the bills.

To change Kim's belief, Danny should have dealt with what she *believes* instead of focusing on changing her *intentions* to pay off bills before the trip.

Affect

In the hierarchal order of persuasive attributes, the next most difficult attribute to change is *affect*. Affect is not just emotion expressed outwardly, like Kim displayed. It's also nonverbal internal emotions.

Neurological scientists have discovered that our brains subconsciously register emotional feelings first. Then those emotional feelings tell your body how to physically respond.[25] Here's how it works.

Effectively, our brains work like a corporate communication system where a switchboard operator is the center of communication. When you see and hear something, the switchboard operator of your brain sends an email to your brain's Department of Archives asking, "What is this and what does it mean?"

Your Department of Archives goes to the subconscious network and searches through your past-experience folders

---

[25] Lehrer, 2009

for any graphic, audio, and *affect* files that match what you just experienced. If what you've seen and heard contains positive affect files, the Department of Archives attaches all the files it found to a reply email and sends it back to the operator. They also add a smiley face signaling to the operator that it is something positive. The operator forwards that email to the rest of the brain with instruction on what each part of the body is to do in response. I call this the "It's all good" email.

Have you ever unexpectedly run into a good friend you haven't spoken to in decades? Upon first sight, the operator queries the Department of Archives. It emails all the historical file attachments and smiley face back to your operator. The operator sends the "It's all good" smiley face email to the rest of the brain, along with instructions on how to respond. Instantly, without thinking about it, your bodily functions respond accordingly. Your eyes open real wide, you start to smile, and you open your arms for a hug. You might even let out an audible shout.

These reactions are unconsciously natural. When you see an old friend, you don't pause for a moment and robotically think: smile, open arm, hug. No. The *affects* you feel from your past experiences with that friend cause your

187

body to unconsciously react before you are aware of what you're doing.

Your *affect* is so deeply tied to your beliefs and value system, persuading your mate to change her *affect* is the second hardest attribute to persuade. The deeper the emotional feeling she has, the more persuasive your message has to be.

As a leader, if you're going to attempt to persuade your mate in one direction, you'd better know what attribute(s) you need to change. Anything dealing with her *beliefs* or *affect* is going to be difficult. Not impossible, but difficult. So if attempted, your persuasive efforts better be top quality, solid, and very convincing. I'll discuss how to climb and conquer this mountain later in this chapter.

Intentions

You've heard someone say, "Think before you act." Well, this is what they were talking about. Your *intentions* are your thoughts. And your *behavior* is the act itself.

Your *intentions* are essentially what you plan to do. And your *behavior* is ultimately what you do. Your *intentions* and your *behavior* are also influenced by your *beliefs* and *affect*.

It works like this: whatever you believe or emotionally feel, you first plan to do something and then you do it— always in that order.

This is true even when you subconsciously react to a stimulus, like a shrieking scream from a baby. In this case, the operator receives a sad face from the Department of Archives. I call this the "It's all bad" email. The operator sends the sad face email to the rest of the brain, along with instructions on how to respond. Immediately, parts of your brain tell your eyes where to look, your legs where to run, and the rest of your body instructions to do whatever it needs to do to get there as fast as possible.

Your response is so quick it's hard to separate the *intent* from your corresponding *behavior*. But they are indeed separate. John-Dylan Haynes, a scientist who studies brain activity, discovered regions toward the front of the brain that store *intentions* until they are executed. Regions in the back of the brain take over when subjects become active and start doing the planning. And additional research identified that our *intentions* for future actions are

189

processed in one part of the brain and then sent to another part of the brain to be executed behavior.[26]

Behavior

It is more difficult to persuade your mate to change her *intent* than it is her *behavior* because her intentions are housed in her past experiences. To try to persuade your mate to change her intentions, you have to know how to inject your preferred approach into her mental pre-calculations. And if you saw the movie *Inception*, with Leo DiCaprio, then you know how difficult that can be. But once you change her intentions, it's a lot easier to change her behavior.

Changing one's *behavior* is the easiest attribute to persuade your mate to change. Why? Because behavioral change takes place at the conscious level. People are more willing to change their *behavior* or actions without you having to change their beliefs, affect, or intentions. People can disassociate their beliefs, feelings, and intentions from their *actions*. We see it all the time in the work environment.

---

[26] Max Planck Society, 2007.
http://www.sciencedaily.com/releases/2007/02/070208131728.htm

When a problem occurs at work, you might change your *behavior* to accommodate what your boss wants you to do, even though you *intended* on solving it differently, or you *feel* your solution is better because your past experiences and value system tell you that your approach is right and acceptable.

Likewise, in a relationship, you are more willing to do something that your mate wants you to do even if you don't want to. We call that compromise. But the act of doing it doesn't mean that you believe it's good, right, or acceptable.

My wife agreed to go whitewater rafting with me while on vacation in Quebec, Canada. And she has a healthy fear of water. It was impossible trying to persuade her to change her beliefs, affect, or intentions about going whitewater rafting. I first tried to convince her with the "It will be fun" approach. That didn't work. So I tried the "You will be safe, I'll protect you" approach. That didn't work either. The only reason she eventually decided to go is because she knew I really wanted to go. So she sacrificed and took one for the team.

And as we were on the rapids, never once did she change her initial belief, affect, or intentions about whitewater rafting, especially when we realized that this was a French speaking group and the guide was only going to speak French. That was the fastest I've ever learned a foreign language.

Danny and Kim Pt. 4: The Message

Previously, on the Danny and Kim saga…fresh off their anniversary vacation, Kim summoned Danny downstairs to listen to a seemingly important voicemail message.

Beep Message #6: "Hello. This message is for Danny. My name is Brian. I'm the executive director of The Childhood Initiative. Several months ago, you submitted a proposal to Dana, our youth program director, about a new mentoring program you developed for our junior high boys and girls. We really liked your ideas. Dana spoke very highly of you and your wife. I'm sorry it took so long for us to get back to you. But we had to secure funding before we could make any commitments in our programs. Initially we wanted bring you and Kim in as the activities coordinators for the boy and girls programs. However, Dana is leaving us. And she recommended you as her replacement for the youth program director position and recommended Kim for the activities coordinator position. Both are part-time positions. I know it's been a long time since you submitted your proposal, but I'd like to talk to you and see if this is something you and Kim are interested in. Give me a call to discuss this further. Oh, and I don't mean to rush you, but we need to make a decision sooner than later because we have our kickoff event coming next month and we need to get the director and coordinator positions filled as soon as possible. Look forward to hearing from you. Good-bye."

Danny and Kim just stand there frozen, staring at each other in a wide-eyed daze.

Beep Message #7: "Hello Danny. It's Brian from The Childhood Initiative. How are you doing? I was trying to reach you a couple days ago to see if you have any interest in the program director position we have available over here, and if Kim would be interested in the activities coordinator position. If so, we are trying to get you both in here before Dana leaves so she can brief you on the plans for the upcoming kickoff event. If you're not interested, let me know one way or the other and we'll go with someone else. But we'd really like you and Kim to lead these programs. Call me back as soon as possible. Thanks. Talk to you soon.

Beep Message #8: "Kim! I know you're on vacation. I didn't want to call you and mess up your vacation but call me as soon as you get home. Mom fell. She was cleaning the kitchen and slipped on some food that fell on the floor. She's alright. Michelle was with her. She didn't want to go to the hospital. But Michelle made her go because she called 911. The paramedics came and said she should have it looked at just in case. You know how Mom is, always trying to downplay stuff. I'm on my way to the hospital now. I'll update you when I find out from the doctor what's going on. Bye."

Danny's mouth drops. Kim buckles over and slowly stumbles into the chair at the kitchen table.

Beep Message #9: "Kim, it's T. The doctor said she didn't break anything. *Thank God!* She did bruise her hip and banged up her elbow pretty bad. They put it in a sling. You know she doesn't like that. She also kept rubbing her knee so they took her back to get X-rays on it. But she's all right. When we get the X-rays back from her knee, if they're negative, they're going to discharge her. Hope you're having a good vacation. I'll leave you another message later once we figure out everything. Okay. Bye."

Kim and Danny both let out a sigh of relief. Kim rummages through her purse and grabs her cell phone.

Beep Message #10: "Hello Danny. It's Brian from The Childhood Initiative. I figured you are out of town or something because I haven't heard back from you. Look, it's Friday, 4:40 p.m. If you are out of town, and you make it back in before Monday, call me on my cell over the weekend. It doesn't matter what time. I need to connect with you before Monday to get a thumbs up or down. Because Monday we have to make a decision. If I don't hear from you by then, we are going to go with someone else. Hope to hear from you soon."

Danny slumps over, slowly shaking his head, as he slides into another chair at the kitchen table.

Beep Message #11: "Hey Kim, this is my last update. Mom's home. The X-ray of her knee came back negative for anything broken. It is swollen though. They wrapped it with an ace-bandage and told her to put some ice on it and keep it elevated. The bad news is that she has a small hairline fracture on her right wrist. The doctor ordered additional X-rays of her wrist when they X-rayed her knee. They put a wrist brace on to stabilize it. She has to go to an orthopedic specialist to have a cast put on. You know she doesn't want to do that. She's going to have limited mobility on her right arm. So me, you, and Michelle are going to have to get together when you get back and talk about what we need to do to be there for Ma because she can't do anything with her right side. Call me when you get back. Okay...bye Kim. Oh...and welcome back!"

A Leader's Persuasive Communication Efforts

Persuasion and Confidence

Communicating a persuasive message has little to do with the actual person communicating the message or the message itself. The most important part of a leader's persuasive communication is confidence.[27]

Your mate is not dumb. She has a mind of her own. Based on her value system, she has accumulated a wide range of BAIBs, which have been backed up and reinforced by her value system and years of past experiences. Based

---

[27] Jaccard, 1981

upon the issue, she has acquired a level of confidence in her own BAIB, ranging from high to low. The more confidence she has in her own BAIB, the more likely she is to reject someone else's.

Persuasion is about shifting one's confidence.[28] Your ability to persuade your mate hinges on whether you can convince your mate to place more confidence in your BAIB than she already has in her own.

Creating a Persuasive Argument: Complex versus Simple Messages

Your ability to persuade, then, is dependent on knowing how to present a persuasive enough argument to make her sway her confidence to your BAIB. That's the key.

"How do I do this?" you ask. Very skillfully.

Your persuasive efforts hinge on knowing what kind of argument (explanation or justification of your proposition, suggestion, or proposal) to make based on the issue at hand.

Knowing and understanding your mate is essential to this. You need to know if she perceives the issue at hand to

---

[28] Jaccard, 1981

be a lower-tier issue, like one affecting her *intentions* or *behavior*, or a higher-tier issue, like one affecting her *beliefs* or *feelings*. Knowing the difference will give you a clue on how simple or complex your persuasive argument has to be.

A simple message is an assertion made with no supporting arguments or evidence. A complex message is an assertion made with supporting arguments and/or evidence. [29]

Higher-Tier Issues Require Complex Messages

How she perceives the issue and what she requires to be convinced to change her BAIB will determine how much detail you need to provide in your persuasive argument. You might even have to come with the whole kitchen sink of facts and figures, historical examples, and expert testimony.

Do you need to present her with a bullet-point message, a summary message, or an all-out detailed plan? The trick is learning how much detail she requires based on how she

---

[29] Jaccard, 1981

perceives the issue. That's something you'll have to learn about her.

Lower-Tier Issues Require a Simple Message

Lower-tier issues that stem from your mate's *behavior* and *intentions* require a simpler and less detailed message. You shouldn't have to print out the Zagat restaurant ratings and a curated restaurant review to persuade your mate to go to Outback's Steakhouse instead of Olive Garden.

But a simple persuasive message doesn't mean no persuasion. You still have to know what specific information is pertinent and how much of it is needed to convince her to exchange her confidence.

One of the best pieces of advice I ever received about marriage, that I didn't fully appreciate until after I got married, was from the Apostle Paul: "Husbands, likewise, dwell with them [your wives] with understanding" (1 Peter 3:7 NKJV). Gaining this understanding helped me avoid a lot of unnecessary confusion, arguments, and drama. Do ye likewise.

It's impossible for me to tell you exactly what to say to persuade your mate on any given issue. Or accurately tell you how much detail to include in every persuasive message on any particular issue. Your job is to know what issues are at play. Know what she *believes* and *feels*. Know what her *intentions* are. And know what she will likely *do*.

Maybe this is where you went wrong in the past. Maybe your message was too simple to sway her confidence. Maybe you pulled a Danny and crafted a simple message for a *belief* issue.

That's why knowing and understanding your mate is so critical. That information will help you craft the right message with the right amount of information she requires in order to exchange her confidence for your BAIB.

If you don't know your mate, then you better start learning her. I remember hearing Dr. Phil say on his TV show that the best predictor of future behavior is past behavior. Begin learning your mate's BAIB by reflecting on what her BAIBs were in previous incidents. Don't worry about what to do after that. By the time you finish this book, you'll know exactly what to do next. But for now, just start learning your mate.

Credible Source

A credible source goes a long way in swaying her confidence. If your mate doesn't believe you are credible, then it's likely she won't replace her confidence in her BAIB with yours. You'd have an easier time kicking a boulder up a hill barefoot than trying to sway a woman to exchange her confidence in a man she perceives has no credibility.

Now she may, at times, reluctantly do what you ask her to do. And with that you will be met with a bunch of questions even on lower-tier issues. But by no means will you ever persuade her to the degree that she has confidence in you as a man she can trust, rely on, or want to follow.

But all is not lost. If you have proven to be less than credible, then start by admitting it. In politics, it's not the scandal that ruins political careers. It's their failure to admit their wrongdoing and the subsequent cover up.

In leadership, humility goes a long way. Admitting your less-than-credible past will potentially give you credibility for being honest and humble. You might also need to apologize for your past missteps. It will lead to increasing your credibility and her willingness to trust, respect and follow you.

Mastering Task-Oriented Goals Develops Her Confidence in You as a Credible Source

Another sure-fire way of improving your credibility is to start solving problems and mastering task-oriented goals. There's no better way to erase the bad than by doing good. It's the classic case of "the good outweighing the bad." But you have to do a lot more good in the near future to make up for all the bad you're done in the past.

Solving problems and mastering task-oriented goals makes you that go-to guy, as one she can trust and respect. If she trusts and respects you, then she'll consider your opinion. After you have shown yourself to be credible over a period of time, then she'll begin to replace her confidence with you on lower-tiered positions. As you learn more about her, learn how to identify her lower- and higher-tier issues. Learn how to craft the appropriate simple and complex messages. Then you'll start to see her exchange her confidence for yours on higher-tier issues.

Confidence and Trust

All this talk about confidence is just a fancy way of describing trust. If you have confidence that someone will behave according to your expectations, then you trust them. If you don't have that confidence, then you don't trust them.

Most people consider trust to be something positive and beneficial to a relationship. However, just like power, trust is neither positive nor negative. Because, based on your BAIB, you can have confidence in the expectation that something good will happen or that something bad will happen. Either way, it's still trust.

My first car was a 1981 five-speed Toyota Corolla Tercel. I loved that car. I also trusted it. I had confidence that my little four-cylinder vehicle didn't have any get-up power. And if I was going to pull out into traffic, my BAIB told me that I need a lot of space and time to catch up with the flow of traffic. Otherwise, I would get rear-ended.

Conversely, I currently have a 2003 eight-cylinder 320hp Yukon Denali XL...with massive get-up. In this vehicle, my BAIB offers me the same level of confidence I had in my Toyota, except I know I can pull into busy traffic and catch up and even surpass the flow of traffic in any given situation with 365 lb-ft of torque under the hood, to my wife's dismay.

In a relationship, this confidence/trust goes both ways too. Your BAIB can give you a high degree of confidence/trust that your mate, given the circumstance, will lose her mind if she finds a good sale on shoes and handbags. Or, based on your history, your wife's BAIB can give her the same degree of confidence/trust that you will lose your mind if you go to Las Vegas with a certain group of friends.

The confidence your mate has in your current persuasive message is based on the credibility you've earned from previous experiences. And based on that, her BAIB gives her a degree of confidence/trust that you will do what she expects you to do, which will either be something beneficial or detrimental to her survival and/or happiness.

This is the formula that determines whether your mate will exchange her confidence for your BAIB, and whether you are able to persuade her in the future. If you meet her expectations, specifically the good ones, you will increase her confidence/trust in you and increase your chances of successfully persuading her.

Need surefire tips on how to earn your woman's trust—or rebuild it after it's been broken? Get this extra content www.HisLeadershipHerTrust.com/thebook.

Now, let's look at Danny's attempts to persuade Kim.

Kim and Danny Pt. 5: Danny Considers the Opportunity

After listening to the last message, Kim abruptly hangs up the phone and immediately calls her mother. "Momma? Are you alright? How are you feeling?

She pauses. Then Kim looks up at Danny and with a sigh, gives him the all-clear head nod. "What happened, Mom?"

She's obviously going to be there for a while. So Danny goes back upstairs to finish unpacking, figuring that he'll get the details from Kim after she finishes talking to her mother. Plus, he had some thinking to do.

"What am I going to do about this opportunity at The Childhood Initiative?" Danny ponders. "This is obviously a great opportunity. But the timing couldn't be worse. Since I haven't heard anything back from them in several months, I've all but given up on working with them. I've moved on to other things."

"But this opportunity was something I really wanted. And this opportunity to be the director makes this an even more interesting opportunity. I can have even more of an impact on the lives of young boys and girls in the community. That's exciting!"

"But this is going to be a huge time commitment for both Kim and I. A part-time job. But the good thing about it is that we will be working together and working in an area where we both are passionate."

"But now there's this issue with Kim's mom. That is bound to change the priority of things around here. And I have to make a decision tonight or the decision will be made for me. But I can't decide anything until I talk this over with Kim and see what's up with her mom and where her head is at. And that is going to be the tricky conversation."

Danny Comes to a Decision

As Danny repeated the same arguments over and over again in his mind, the feeling he was having was that he wanted to do it. But all the cons were making him feel hesitant about moving forward.

He thought to himself, "If I can address these cons, then I'll do it. And the first con I have to overcome is to see if Kim is on board. If I can address any barriers Kim has, then we just have to negotiate the rest of them with Brian."

"Okay. Now that that's settled, I've got to talk to Kim. Given the issue with her mother, I need to first find out what happened with her mother and what she and her sisters are going to work out. After she gives me all the details with that situation, then we can talk about this opportunity."

Danny's Conversation with Kim

After Danny finishes unpacking, he checks to see if Kim is still on the phone. Of course she is. Now she is on a three-way with her sisters. He can tell because she's talking extremely loud and at a pitch she only reserves for intense conversations with her sisters. Danny smartly stays upstairs and gives her more time.

Anticipating Kim will want to tell Danny all the details and then unpack, which will push their conversation about the opportunity late into the evening, Danny unpacks her clothes and puts her stuff away too.

An hour later, Kim gets off the phone and comes upstairs. She plops down on the bed and lets out a big moan. "Welcome home," Danny says jokingly. "So what happened? How's your mother?"

That's all it took for Kim to begin spewing out all the details, plots, back stories, who did what, who said what, you wouldn't believe this and that, etc. Danny just sits there and listens, with an occasional question or comment.

Forty minutes pass. The more Kim recounts the conversations, the more tired and emotionally drained she grows. As the hour grew later and evening turned into night, Danny tries to figure out a way to transition to his topic of choice. He has an idea.

Danny was looking for an opening, like a girl jumping double-dutch trying to get in when there's someone already in the middle. Danny was looking for a way to ask a question about how often Kim is going to go over to her mother's to check on her. So Danny waits till she reaches that point in their conversation. Kim starts to tell him the who, what, and when about checking on her mother. Danny interrupts her before she could speak.

"Oh yeah, while I was unpacking your stuff and thinking about the Childhood Initiative opportunity, I was wondering what y'all would decide about checking on your mother. What did you all come up with?"

Kim paused. "You put my stuff away? Aw, thanks honey. I was dreading that." She paused again. "I'm going over to Ma's house tomorrow and Tuesday. Michelle is going to take her to the orthopedic specialist Wednesday. After that we'll know more about it—if she has to wear a cast, how long she'll have to wear it, and so on. Tracey will go over there the rest of the week and we'll all probably go over there on the weekends. But after Wednesday, we'll know more about her limitations and whether she'll have to wear the cast."

"Well, that's good," Danny says empathetically.

There was a brief moment of silence. Then Kim remembers what Danny said about the Childhood Initiative opportunity. "What were your thoughts on the Childhood Initiative thing? You said you were thinking about that, because, to be honest, I don't know. With mom and everything...I just don't know. Plus they took forever getting back to us. What do they think? We'd just sit around and wait for them to get back to us?"

Danny interrupts her again. "Let's talk about that in a minute. Go ahead and change your clothes and get comfortable. I'm going to get something to eat. You want anything?" Danny says as he's leaving the room.

"Yes. Heat up a frozen pizza," Kim replies. "I'll be down in a few."

Analysis of Danny's Actions

Danny is a smart man. Why? Because he completed the first step of leadership: initiating roles. Remember, initiating roles is the process of assessing the scope of the problem or task-oriented goal, assigning roles, and initiating the discussion. These three steps all take place before you say a single word to your mate. It's the conversation you have with yourself. It's you, sorting out what you really want to do, how you think it should be done, and preparing the right place and time to discuss it with your mate. And that's exactly what Danny did.

Assess the scope

With all the opportunities, options, and possibilities he had to choose from, Danny took the time while unpacking to think through his thoughts about the pros and cons of this opportunity. He didn't have all the answers. And he didn't need to at that point. Just giving serious thought to all the possibilities was good enough. Because it helped him think through the impact of all the possible options. This will prove beneficial when he actually has the conversation with Kim.

Assigned roles: determine roles and responsibilities

Assigning roles, in this instance, was not too difficult, given Brian already mentioned what roles he wanted Danny and Kim to take. However, it doesn't mean that as a leader, you can neglect your responsibility to assign roles yourself. Be very careful about letting someone else define what role you will play, even if it has to do with an employment opportunity. You still have 100 percent control of the access to and distribution of your time.

Brian is using his power resources as the executive director to control the access to resources (a job), finances (the finances that go along with the job) and time (the time frame that Danny has to call him back). But Danny and Kim have power resources too—human resources, information, and time. Danny and Kim should not approach this decision from a position of, "Should we take this job?" That is a position of powerlessness. Rather, they should approach it from a position of, "They want our human resources, information, and time. How do we want to utilize these resources at the Childhood Initiative and at what price?" That is a position of power.

Danny and Kim don't have to accept the limitations Brian has placed on their roles and responsibilities. Instead, they should determine their roles for themselves. Even if they choose the same roles offered to them, it's Danny and Kim who are determining how they want to use their own power resources, not Brian.

Initiate the Discussion

Initiating the discussion is not necessarily about what you say, but when and where you say it. In Danny's opinion, the time and place where they would have this conversation was key. He set it up perfectly—after Kim had a chance to talk to her mother and sisters; after Kim told Danny all the details of her conversation with her family; and after Kim changed her clothes and got comfortable.

What do you think would have happened if Danny tried to discuss this job opportunity with her before she talked to her family, or before the she told him all the details of her conversation?

What if Danny would have been like, "Hey, I waited hours for you to get off the phone. Before we go into what's going on with your mother, let's talk about this opportunity at the Childhood Initiative." It would be a disaster. Kim would reject it outright because her priority was to first make sure her family situation was addressed. Then she would be emotionally freed up to discuss all other matters of lesser importance to her.

These small nuances may seem insignificant or trivial, especially in the larger scope of leadership in an organizationally structured relationship. Some might think, "Who cares where you have the discussion? I'm going to say what I need to say when I need to say it." Well, okay, Mr. "My Way" Man. If you want to deliver your persuasive message like that—without any prep, without properly initiating the discussion—then be prepared to receive the same kind of unconcerned, insensitive response from your mate.

Also, be prepared for a future response to lack consideration for the kind of stressful day you've had. Be prepared for her to always discuss her issues first before you can discuss yours. Just be prepared for any one of these selfish traits to resurface at the most inopportune time.

Danny's Use of Power

Danny also did something else. Did you catch it? Can you figure out which TRIPAR power resources he used? If you said time and information, you're pretty good. You're catching on. If you also said affect, then you're really good. Let's examine.

When Danny interrupted Kim and went downstairs to make the pizza, he was effectively using his power to control when (*time*) he was going to share his thoughts (*information*) with Kim. And he did it in a way that controlled Kim's emotions (*affect*). By telling her to get comfortable and asking her if she wanted something to eat, it softened his abrupt shutting down of the conversation. He was controlling the environment (*affect*) under which they would have this discussion.

See, Danny didn't want Kim all riled up, just coming off an emotional exasperating recounting of her conversation with her family. He didn't want those emotions (*affect*) to carry into his conversation. He wanted to create a calm, relaxed environment.

Danny's Attempt to Persuade Kim: The Process of Influence

Kim changes. The pizza is finally ready. Even though Kim said she was going to come downstairs, Danny brings the whole pizza, plates, napkins, and two beverages upstairs to the bedroom. How sweet, right?

Yes, and how strategic. The comfy clothes and cozy bedroom is a much better environment to have this discussion than the cold sterile kitchen.

Danny and Kim grab a slice and sit on the bed. Kim dives in. She's starving. Danny is chewing and thinking…thinking and chewing. He swallows and sips his beverage.

"So this Childhood Initiative gig—interesting, huh?" Danny asks rhetorically. Kim wrinkles her nose as she continues to chew. "Here are my thoughts about it. Months ago, we put this proposal together with the expectation to work as the program coordinators. They took a long time getting back to us. I know we are just off a vacation, you have to tend to your mom, and who else knows what will come up tomorrow. But my initial desire to work as program coordinator is still there. It hasn't waned with the passing of time, although I'm a little irritated that it took so long for them to get back to us. But regardless of how long it took them, I still want to do it."

"But they are asking you to be the program director and me to be the activities coordinator," Kim adds, "which is not what we originally signed up for. I don't know…"

"That was my next point," Danny interrupts, anticipating Kim was about to hijack his pitch. "Just because they asked me to be the director doesn't mean I have to accept that position. If I don't want the director position, I don't feel obligated to take it."

"That said," he continues, "when I look at the idea of being the activities coordinator with no program director above me, I'll be doing my own thing as a coordinator anyway. Then having Brian hire a new program director and they'll come in and take over. And I'll have to switch gears and do whatever this new director wants to do. That would probably frustrate me. I like the programs Dana put together. For someone else to come in there, I don't know if I'd like that. So the idea of me being the director is not a turnoff. I would definitely have to ask Brian some questions and see how much authority, flexibility, and money I would have. But I'm not totally against the idea. What do you think?"

Lesson 1 of 1: Communicate and Wait

I'm going to interrupt Danny's pitch for a teachable moment. Lesson number one of one in communication and leadership in relationships: Communicate and wait.

Communicate your thoughts and then wait for feedback. I wanted to drive home the point that there's only one lesson for you to learn in this section.

Don't just ramble on. Stop and get feedback throughout your pitch/argument/presentation. Communicating and waiting gives you a chance to see where her head is. Is she still persuadable? Is she already in agreement with your position? Or is she clinging on to her confidence in her own BAIB?

And depending on her BAIB, this opportunity is either a lower-tier issue—something just affecting her *intentions* or *behavior*, or a higher-tier issue—something affecting her more strongly held *beliefs* or *feelings*. You need to know which one it is!

Your ability to persuade her relies on knowing how strong a case you need to make. Her feedback will give you the information you need to adjust your message to a simple or more complex message on the fly to sway her confidence in your direction.

Danny Attempts to Persuade Kim: The Process of Influence Continues

Kim responds. "I don't know. I've just got a lot of stuff on my mind." She pauses. "My mother is hurt. I've got to go over there several times a week to make sure she has everything she needs. I just don't know."

"This is something I wanted to do too," she continues. "But timing is everything. We also need to know what this director position entails. And what does the program coordinator position look like? What's going to be the difference between your position and mine? How much time is going to be involved? Because my mom is a priority." She pauses again. "I just don't know if I can give it my all at this time. I don't know." She finishes with a blank stare, holding her glass up close to her mouth but not taking a sip.

Danny quietly takes a deep breath, letting the silence punctuate his respect for her feelings. Danny now knows that this issue is more than a lower-tiered *behavior* issue to Kim. It seems to be a mixture of *belief, affect* and *intention*. So he automatically knows he has to come with a much more complex argument to sway her confidence. He needs

219

supporting evidence to help him make his case. Let's see what happens next:

Nodding his head, Danny replies, "I agree. You're right. There is a lot going on right now. And there's a lot about this opportunity we don't know. And I think we should find out the answers to these questions so we can make a decision about this. I don't want to decide not to do it, when it's something we wanted to do and it's something we would be great at, until we get answers to those questions. So let's do this..."

Danny picks up his cell phone and dials a number. "Who are you calling?" Kim asks. Danny doesn't respond. Danny puts the phone to his ear.

"Hello Brian, this is Danny. Looks like we're playing phone tag. I apologize for just getting back to you. You were right, we were out of town. Just got back in this evening. This opportunity sounds very interesting, but you kinda switched gears on us," he says with a chuckle. "We have some competing priorities on our end, but we definitely would like to talk to you about what all this entails and whether this is something that would be a good fit for both of us. Give me a call as soon as you get this message. Kim and I are up talking about this right now and we've got some questions. Hopefully you can answer them so we can make a decision. Hopefully tonight. If not, then definitely by tomorrow before you make your final decision. Talk to you soon."

Danny hangs up. "Okay, Kim. Now let's see what Brian says."

"What if he doesn't call you back tonight?" Kim asks.

"He said call him anytime. If he doesn't call me back, then…oh well…he must not want the Dynamic Duo," Danny says with a chuckle. Kim returns a half-hearted smirk.

"Kim," Danny continues, "what is our bottom line?"

"What do you mean? How much are they paying us?"

"Not just pay, but everything else. Right now, you're leaning toward not taking it. Well, what are the conditions you must have in order to say 'Okay, let's do it. This is a great opportunity!' That's our bottom line."

"Oh, well…let me think about it," she replies.

For several minutes, Kim and Danny roll off approximately five to seven things that would make this an opportunity of the century for them. As they were finishing up their conversation, Danny's cell phone rings. It's Brian.

"Hi, Danny. It's Brian. Thanks for calling me back. Hope you had a good trip."

Kim puts her glass on the nightstand and moves close to Danny. Danny put the phone on speaker so Kim can participate. They exchange warm pleasantries before getting down to business.

"So Brian...Kim and I were just talking about you."

"I hope it was good," Brian added.

"It depends. Either you're my hero with the greatest opportunity in the world for us, or you're the Grinch who stole Christmas." They all laugh. "So tell me about what's going on at the Childhood Initiative."

Brian proceeds to tell them about all the changes that have taken place since they last spoke. He talks about Dana's departure for a new job, the new grant funding, plans for the upcoming year, and the new positions and responsibilities. Danny and Kim ask a ton of questions. Commitment questions, which answer Kim's questions about how much of her time this will take up. Authority questions, which address the level of authority Danny will have to set up and run the programs the way he wants. Bottom line questions, which answer Danny and Kim's conditions that would make this the opportunity of a lifetime.

They conclude their conversation with Brian. Danny promises Brian they will discuss it amongst themselves and call him back with a response before 9:00 am. After Danny hangs up, they both take a deep breath.

Lesson 1 of 1 (revisited): Communication and Wait

I'm going to interrupt this story again to revisit lesson number 1 of 1: Communicate and wait. Seek information first, rather than assume she is convinced one way or another. You are still looking for clues to see where her head is at, and what kind of persuadable message you need to craft to sway her confidence.

Even if you think the information presented should be enough to persuade her, you don't *know* what she's thinking at this point. Remember, her history, value system, belief, and subconscious emotions will dictate how she feels about what she just heard. Your thoughts about what you heard, however right you think they are, will likely be different from hers. So, again, seek first to gain information, rather than trying to persuade. Communicate and wait.

Danny and Kim Discuss Their Options

Danny looks at Kim. "So what are your thoughts?" Danny probes.

"Uh," Kim pauses for a moment. "What Brian said was good and all, but my first priority right now is taking care of my mom. I don't see how we can do this at this point in time or at least, how *I* can do it."

Now Danny knows what Kim is thinking. She has not been convinced. But that's okay. He now knows he needs to address Kim's concern at the point of her belief. To persuade her, he's going to have to use his power to control the TRIPAR in their relationship. Watch how he does it.

"So what you're saying," Danny pauses as he picks up his glass and takes a sip, "is that you don't think the time is right because you have to care for your mother? Would that be accurate?"

"Pretty much," Kim answers. She adds, "I mean, you can do it. I know this is something you've wanted to do. And I don't want to say you can't do it because I can't do it right now. So you can do it. I just—"

"No!" Danny interrupts. "That's not how I wanted to do this. I want to do this with you. We're going to do this together or not do it at all."

"Well, I don't know how we are going to do that since—"

"I have an idea," Danny says, cutting her off. "I have an idea that will work for you. It will allow you to care for your mother and allow us to both take advantage of this opportunity right now."

"Oh yes? Let's hear it, Mr. Bright Ideas."

"OK. Listen."

"I'm listening."

"OK, wait a minute. OK…here it is. Your main concern is caring for your mother, right? And my position is for the program director and yours is for the activities coordinator, right?"

Kim looks at him with a wide-eyed stare like "Duh!" He continues. "Well, I can set your schedule to accommodate whatever you need to do for your mother. Think about it. Whatever arrangements you establish with your sisters, your schedule will revolve around your availability. And in the case of the upcoming activities The Childhood Initiative already has scheduled for next month, you can coordinate those dates with your sisters in advance to make sure your mom is covered. And if something suddenly comes up and you need to get away, we can just deal with those situations as they arrive, with the understanding that your mother is *our* top priority. Does this address your concerns, Kim?"

Let's revisit lesson number 1 of 1 again: Communicate and wait. State your case, then *shut up*! Do not over-pitch your point. Let the silence of the moment punctuate your point. The worst thing you could do is try to fill the dead air with further explanations of why she should go with your idea. You need her feedback to gauge where she is.

Back to the story.

Kim sits quietly in deep contemplation. Danny says nothing. He's in shut up mode.

"Well...Danny..." Kim utters. She pauses for a long time as she goes through all of her scenarios for any gaps in his plan. "…that might work."

Kim then begins to ask a series of "what if" questions to allay her concerns and gain clarity and some reassurance. She wants to make sure every possible scenario is considered. Danny answers all her questions, which are mostly concerns that have already been addressed.

With no further objections, Kim makes her decision. "Well, I guess we can give it a try and see how it works out."

"You sure?"

"Yes, I guess. We can give it a try."

"Cool. I'll call Brian back and let him know our decision. I'll let him know that this is contingent upon me having the flexibility to adjust your schedule to care for your mother."

Danny calls Brian and informs him of their decisions. Brian is very understanding about the flexible scheduling condition. He agrees to it. They negotiate over pay and agree to amicable terms. Danny and Kim agree to start in two weeks to the glee of all parties.

How Did Danny Persuade Kim?

After Danny and Kim spoke to Brian and had all their questions answered, Danny was wise to wait for Kim's feedback. Even though Brian was the one who communicated, Danny recognized that he still needed to get feedback from Kim based on what Brian said. By waiting for feedback, he was able to gauge where her head was at. That's when he discovered that her confidence was firmly embedded in her *intentions* and *beliefs*.

It was not a problem. That just called for a more complex message to sway her confidence. And that's when Danny reached into his power resources bag of tools and pulled out his control over *affect*, *time*, and *resources* (*human resources*).

Affect

Control of *affect* in a relationship is arguably the most important power resource to control. Because the emotional *affect* of the parties involved in a discussion can directly impact the outcome of the persuasive effort, regardless of how strong a case the persuader makes.

It follows the old saying, "It's not what you say but how you say it." You can say the right thing and have all the best intentions. But if you say it with an attitude or with a condescending tone, you might as well forget about persuading her, no matter how complex your message is. She will buck you just out of spite.

Danny avoided this catastrophe. He very well could have got in his feelings and start barking orders. He could've huffed and puffed and made his case with an aggravated tone. All of these likely would have caused Kim to shut down. Or like with the issue of saving extra money for their vacation, she could have started a fight with him. Then their wonderful vacation would have ended in a huge argument.

But none of this happened. Danny was calm and measured. He set a calm and peaceful environment. He brought Kim some food and a beverage. He insisted that they have the conversation about The Childhood Initiative opportunities in the comfort of their bedroom, in comfortable clothes.

These may seem like insignificant things. But when talking about sensitive issues, like the care of Kim's mother and a job opportunity that's going to drastically change the schedule of their family for the foreseeable future, every calming effect helps. Look at it this way—even if it doesn't help, it definitely won't hurt. So hedge your bets and err on the side of helping your cause as much as possible.

Another thing Danny did was to stay calm throughout the entire conversation. He didn't flare up when Kim initially didn't want to take the job. He remained cool and collected even when she wasn't convinced after Brian answered all their questions.

He didn't get irritated when Kim asked him all those questions. And he didn't get an attitude when Kim gave a lukewarm agreement to do it, stating, "Yeah, I guess. We can give it a try." Danny didn't get mad, or press her for a more hearty response or acceptance. His goal was to persuade her to agree that both of them would take the job. Mission accomplished, now move on.

In the real world, staying cool and not getting irritated in a situation like this is harder than it looks. That's why knowing what to expect in the process of influencing is so important.

Staying cool and calm in seemingly frustrating situations is not about ensuring you get the outcome expected, but about adjusting your expectation of how you'll get it. Knowing that her reluctance and/or resistance will always be a part of the process of influencing her, you must adjust your expectations to embrace this resistance. You don't have to like it. You just have to know it exists and it will always be a part of your persuasive efforts, regardless of how credible you are or how strong your argument is. And that's because you're dealing with someone's confidence in their own BAIB. Your fighting against a lifetime of beliefs and the affects that go along with it.

And also know...control of the *affect* in a relationship gives you the freedom and flexibility to control any other power resource. In fact, your ability to control *affect* is a power resource itself. The better you are able to control the emotional ups and downs during a conversation, discussion, or whatever, the better chance you have at persuading and leading your group toward solving that problem or accomplishing that goal, and subsequently leading the relationship as a whole.

Time and Resources (Human)

Controlling your own time is more difficult than you expect. There are only 24 hours in a day. If you calculate the time it takes you to get from home to work, door-to-door, that's about 10-12 hours. Add in the time you wake till you leave for work, that's one hour. If you have kids, that's two hours.

If you have kids, you know time spent with them is like rolling the dice in a game of craps. Depending on how many you have, their age, the day of the week, the month of the year, and what activities they're in, you could literally crap-out on any given night.

All totaled, you may only end up with two to four hours of your own time that you actually control before your body takes control and shuts itself down for sleep. If you're anything like me, to gain more control of my own time, you learn to function on three to five hours of sleep. I've just bought myself two more hours of my own time to control. That bumps me up to a whopping 25 percent of my own time to wield as I see fit.

With such time limitations, controlling your own time is a learned skill because you grow up having 100 percent of your time controlled by your parents and teachers. When you leave home, you gain some freedom to control your time as you see fit. But the concept of managing your own time is something you have to learn. And if you don't learn how to control your own time, someone or something else will gladly control it for you: social organizations, nonprofits, churches, charities, friend, girlfriends, wives, children, and the list goes on. And you gladly hand over control of your time for things that you value. Money is a big one. The Childhood Initiative is one for Danny and Kim's. It's requesting access to and control over the distribution of their time and human resources.

However Danny did not just jump at the opportunity. But with great pause, he negotiated their time to make it optimal for Kim's situation. He negotiated the use of their human resources so that Danny had the maximum freedom to manage the program activities as he determined.

He was willing to risk this highly valued opportunity because he placed more value on their time and resources than the money they would earn and satisfaction of having his proposal accepted.

Because Brian highly valued the resources Kim and Danny would bring to the Childhood Initiative, he yielded to their requirement.

As people vie for your time, your skill sets (information), and other power resources your time brings, make sure you negotiate your power resources from the position of how much you feel your power resources are worth, instead of how much someone is willing to give you for them. Otherwise, you run the risk of pimping yourself out and handing control of your ever-decreasing time and accumulated power resources to someone or something else.

Power, Persuasion, and Influence

Being the leader in a relationship is not as easy as it seems. There are so many moving parts you have to be aware of, both tangible and intangible. As the leader, you are responsible for managing all of them. You don't have to do it all. You don't even have to know it all. But you are responsible for it all.

When Adam and Eve ate the fruit in the Garden of Eden, God didn't go to Eve and say, "Have you eaten from the tree I commanded you not to eat from?" No. He went straight to Adam. Even though Eve ate the fruit first then gave it to Adam, he was the one God held responsible for both of their transgressions.

So it is with you too, sir. Being the leader of your relationship is your responsibility.

How do you do it? Well, it starts with understanding the process of influence. This two-step process involves using the power resources you've accumulated, which is the way you control TRIPAR, to persuade your mate to place more confidence in your proposed BAIB than the BAIB she already has.

You do this by initiating a plan, communicating it to her, then shutting up and waiting for her response. Depending on how strong her confidence is in her own BAIB, that determines how simple or complex an argument you need to make to sway her confidence in your favor and persuade her.

That's it. That's all you have to do. This is the essence of what this book is about: what to do and say to provide leadership. Easy, right?

Like I said earlier, leadership is a lot harder than it sounds. Many men's relationships have bled and died on the battlefield of influence, power, and persuasion, all in a pursuit of leadership. Some men had a wealth of power resources, but didn't know how to use them without misusing or abusing it. Some men didn't use it enough and showed themselves to be impotent in the eyes of their mate.

Other men could craft a strong complex persuasive argument but never swayed their mate's confidence because he couldn't tolerate her resistance or continued questioning. He would get frustrated and just shut down. Or some men just did it their way, by himself—Frank Sinatra style.

I hope this information will stave off the plight taken by many men before you. Or I hope you do not repeat any missteps you've taken in the past. Get to know your mate as best you can.

Learn "why" your mate says what she says and does what she does. Inevitably, it all originates back to experiences in her past, when she learned what's right and wrong, good and bad, acceptable and unacceptable.

If you can find out the "why," then you can figure out what kind of arguments you need to craft in order to persuade her to go with your BAIB. Once you come to a point of agreement, like Danny and Kim did, then you move on to the next steps in the leadership process.

Get personal coaching on how to use your power to persuade with Heath Wiggins. Connect with him personally: www.HisLeadershipHerTrust.com/thebook.

These last two steps go hand and glove with each other because they are iterative steps in a repetitive cycle. These last two steps are also the easiest, compared to the first two. The last two steps are execute and check-in.

Chapter 9:

Step 3: Execute Judgment & Decision-Making

Execution is About Judgment and Decision-Making

Now that you know about initiating roles and the discussion, and you've learned how to communicate and wait for feedback from your mate, now it's time to—in the words of Larry the Cable Guy—"Git r done!" It's time to execute your strategy.

Simply put, to *execute* is carrying out what you and your mate decided to do. From painting a living room over the weekend to directing a community-based nonprofit program, executing your plans require the use of good judgment. And good judgment translates into good decisions. For, *a decision is nothing more than executed judgment.*

Whenever I speak to a group of couples about leadership in a relationship, the conversation always pivots off leadership (in general) and focuses like a laser on the man's judgment and decision-making. We then spend the rest of the time talking about his questionable judgment and suspect decision-making, and how they affect her willingness to follow him in the future.

If you have poor judgment and make bad decisions that negatively affects your mate, you'll face all sorts of questions. She'll second-guess your judgment and decisions at every turn, because she doesn't trust you, and her respect for you is fleeting.

She's in self-preservation mode. She's protecting herself from you. Your leadership will suffer because you won't be able to persuade her to give up her confidence in her BAIB.

So your job is to make sure you use good judgment when making decisions so she will trust you, respect you, and be willing to follow you.

The Decision-Making Process

People Make Different Decisions with the Same Information

The decision-making process is the same for mostly everyone. But at the same time, two people can make two different decisions with the same information and circumstances. Take for example Danny's decision to accept the position versus Kim's initial decision to reject it. The process by which they made their decisions was the same, but their final decisions were different.

Reflect on your current and/or previous relationships. Have you ever wondered why the two of you could look at the same information from the same source and come up with two different decisions? And it's not because she's crazy.

The Complexity of the Decision-Making Process

Understanding why people make different decisions about the same information is sometimes confusing, especially when your choice is the most obvious to you. Its complexity comes from all of the different mental and emotional factors you have to consider when making a decision.

Researcher Mark Rogerson[30] found that early research into ethical decision-making tried to prove it was organized into steps that people follow in an orderly fashion. Well, they failed.

---

[30] Rogerson, et al, 2011

Conflicting research poked holes in that theory. Their research concluded that ethical decision-making is a carefully blended cocktail of one's personal values, emotional sensitivity, situational context, time constraints, individual perceptions and biases, intuitive responses, relationships, and rational analysis. Trying to create an ethical decision-making model was nearly impossible because there are too many different variables to consider.

Become an Expert Decision-Maker

So as you can see, trying to come up with a foolproof way to make good decisions is impossible, but what I can do is teach you how to become an expert decision-maker.

What's the difference? The difference is, I'm taking the focus off the decisions you make, and putting it on *you*, the person who's making the decision.

For, if I can teach you how to become an expert decision-maker, then, regardless what internal or external factors make up your cocktail, you will likely be able to make the right decision

From Novice to Expert

In the 1980s, brothers Stuart and Hubert Dreyfus set out on a mission to advance the science of artificial intelligence by creating a software program that studied the way humans learn and acquire skills. They developed what's known as the Dreyfus model of skill acquisition.[31] They researched the learning capability of new language learners, chess players, and airplane pilots. What they uncovered was and still is the benchmark pathway for how to go from being a novice to an expert.

They highlight a five-stage development process. The difference between each stage is the degree to which one follows and adheres to rules. The five stages are the following:

1. **Novice**: You unconditionally follow all the rules, no exceptions.

2. **Advanced Beginner**: You begin creating and identifying situational rules instead of unconditional rules.

---

[31] Dreyfus and Dreyfus, 1980

3. **Competence**: You recognize recurring patterns in the situational rules and start following principles and guidelines.

4. **Proficiency**: Because of your experience, you can recall similar situations and principles you used in the past to help guide you on how to deal with a current situation. You know what information can be ignored and what information is important for making a decision.

5. **Expert**: Your experience is so vast that each situation has an automatic corresponding decision/action associated with it. You don't have to think about what to do.

Becoming an Expert Through Learning

To become an expert decision-maker you have to make mistakes.[32] Errors and mistakes give you an opportunity to learn what *not* to do. The more you learn from your errors and mistakes, the more of an expert you'll become. On the other hand, the more you play it safe and try to avoid making errors and mistakes, or fail to learn from the ones you make, the longer you will stay a novice.

---

[32] Campitellli and Gobet, 2010

Take a rookie NFL football quarterback, for example. It doesn't matter if you were picked #1 in the NFL draft, how much you memorized the playbook, or the amount of film you studied. Until you get some actual reps in practice, make mistakes, and learn what not to do, you will remain a novice with no experience.

The Learning Process: Intuition and Judgment

There has been much theoretical debate about how humans learn.[33] The most widely accepted learning process is the dual process of intuition and judgment.[34] Most people know what these two words mean. But what you probably don't know is how they mysteriously, yet beautifully work together to create the process for how we learn.

Intuition

We experience the world through our five senses...right? For the purpose of this explanation, I'm going to refer to these five sensory experiences as stimuli.

Although the reality of our five senses is undeniable, some people also recognize a mystical, intangible sixth

---

[33] Kahneman and Tversky, 1979
[34] Reynolds, 2006

sense by which they also experience stimuli. Some describe it as a gut feeling. Athletes may describe it as instincts. Cops may refer to it as a hunch. And the faith-based Christian community at times refers to it as the Holy Spirit. The fact is, all of the above may be true. Psychologists call this mystical sixth-sense "intuition."

But what is it? Is it real? Where does it come from? And how does it help you learn?

Simply put, intuition is the *affect* files (feelings) the operator received from the Department of Archives. Its purpose is to help you make decisions without thinking or analyzing any stimuli.

Remember the example in chapter 8 when I asked if you have ever unexpectedly run into a good friend you haven't spoken to in decades. Intuition is the feelings you have that makes you react the way you do.

In that instance, you knew who the person was. But what if you met someone you couldn't remember? That happened to me recently.

I was walking to the subway on my way home from work. A woman stopped me and said, "I know you from somewhere." I looked up at her and I recognized her face, but I couldn't remember where I knew her from. As we were trying to figure out where we knew each other from, my intuition was warning me, 'You don't know her from school, work, or church. Don't pursue this any further.' I had an eerie feeling in my stomach. So I cut it short, said my goodbyes, and continued on my way to the subway.

Judgment

1. Analysis

As I was sitting on the train, I was racking my brain trying to figure out who she was. Or, should I say, my operator was trying to analyze all the attachment files sent from the Department of Archives.

When my intuition is incomplete, that's when my operator uses a variety of factors to consciously analyzing all the stimuli I experienced: my intuition results, context, person's features, sight, sound, smell, etc. My operator is trying to come to a conclusion…to make a judgment.

2. Making a Judgment

About 20 minutes later, my operator completed its analysis. Suddenly it hit me. My intuition was right. I didn't know her from school, work, or church. I knew her from my single tomfoolery and hijinks days. It's a good thing we both didn't remember where we knew each other from. It would have been quite awkward.

Your judgment is the conclusion you arrive at after analyzing your intuition and all the stimuli you've experienced. Your judgment, therefore, is more important than your actual decisions because your decisions are merely the execution of your judgment.

It's your executed judgment that directly impacts your family. Thus, it's your executed judgment that your leadership is judged by. Your mate looks at your past decisions and analyzes them against what you're currently trying to persuade her to do. Then she makes her own judgment whether you're a good leader and whether it's good, right, appropriate, and acceptable for her survival and happiness to give up her confidence in her BAIB for what you're offering and follow you.

Good Judgment = An Expert Decision-Maker

Some people only analyze information at a very superficial level. Others can dig deeper into the true purpose and meaning of things. Thus, your judgment is only as good as your operator's ability to analyze information. And your analysis is only as good as your intuition. And your intuition is only as good as your understanding of your feelings about past experiences. And your feelings are only as good as the past experiences stored in your long term memory, your Department of Archives.

So, if you've had little-to-no past experiences in, let's say, providing leadership in your past relationships, then your intuition on being a leader in your current relationship will be inaccurate. And you'll just do whatever you feel is best at the time.

If your intuition is inaccurate, then your analysis will be flawed because you're analyzing incomplete information.

If you analysis is flawed, then your judgment will be unsound because you've determined what you're going to do based on flawed analysis of inaccurate information.

So by the time your unsound and inaccurate judgment becomes a decision, you are nowhere near being an expert decision-maker. You're definitely a novice!

If you want to become an expert decision-maker, if you're going to be the leader and solve problems in your relationship, then you must have some quality experiences solving problems in a relationship. Otherwise, like the example above, you'll just be making it up as you go along.

And that doesn't instill confidence in your mate for solving problems in the future. In fact, she may decide to take over and start solving the problems herself. And in so doing, you sir, have just been jacked of your position of leadership.

Strong Intuition = Little-to-No Analysis

Those who are expert decision-makers have a high degree of confidence in their intuition. You know who you are. You know what you believe. You have strong core values. You generally hold tightly to them, regardless of the circumstance. This self-awareness gives you the confidence to believe in yourself.

If you have such a strong confidence in your beliefs and value system, then you can accurately identify how you're feeling about a specific stimuli. You won't feel the need to second guess yourself. You won't feel the need to override your intuition after analysis of new information. Because over time, you've learned what is good and bad, right and wrong, acceptable and unacceptable by making and correcting your mistakes and errors.

This produces highly accurate feelings, which get stored in the subconscious network in your Department of Archives. So when called upon again by a new stimuli, the Department of Archives search results will be so detailed and accurate, that your operator won't need to do much analysis, if any at all. And this frees up your operator to analyze new stimuli that you've never encountered before. And that experience creates new memories and feelings that get stored in your Department of Archives for future retrieval.

The Greatest Learning Comes From Blank Emails With No Attachments

We have the greatest opportunity to learn when we experience something new. It's like receiving a blank email from our Department of Archives with no attachments. There are no historical records for this stimulus.

A blank email with no attachments is like a computer error message to our brains that says, "Something is wrong. I don't know what this is. Let me figure it out." Our brains now have to use our analysis and judgment to figure out what it is.

Again, you will use an untold number of factors to analyze what it is. But whatever your final judgment is, right or wrong, those results will be stored in your long-term memory for future reference. And those results, good or bad, are used to define your value system and beliefs.

Expert Decision-Maker

Expert Decision-Maker = Strong Intuition

So the more secure you are with your feelings, the more your intuition can answer life's questions about your encounters with various stimuli. That's when you start approaching expert status.

Experts live and breathe on making judgments with their intuition. An expert's intuition is based on years of doing things the wrong way and their ability to understand what their emotions are telling them about their judgments. Jonah Lehrer[35] explains:

"When an expert evaluates the situation, he doesn't systematically compare all the available options or consciously analyze the relevant information. He doesn't rely on elaborate spreadsheets or long lists of pros and cons. Instead, the expert naturally depends on the emotions generated by his dopamine neurons. His prediction errors have been translated into useful knowledge, which allows him to tap into a set of accurate feelings he can't begin to explain."

When an expert uses their intuition to make judgments instead of having to use their analysis, it frees up their brain to quickly analyze new stimuli. Because their brain isn't pulling double-duty—analyzing both past experiences and new ones—they are more agile at making decisions.

You can analyze new experiences and make judgments quicker, more efficiently, and naturally. This combination of a strong intuition and a quick reactive analysis of new stimuli makes you an expert decision-maker.

---

[35] Jonah Lehrer (2009, pg. 54)

Novice Decision-Maker = Poor Judgment

On the opposite side of the spectrum is the poor decision-maker. People don't make poor decisions in a vacuum.

If you are unsure or insecure about your beliefs and value system, then you will be insecure about your feelings. If you're inexperienced in the area in which you are making judgments, then your intuition will be inaccurate. This will cause you to make errors in your analysis of your intuition. Ultimately your judgment and decisions will be errant.

This person is a novice. He doesn't have the experience in his long-term memory from which to draw; and/or his intuition, analysis, and/or judgment are incorrect. I don't care how old you are or how many years of experience you have doing anything—if you can't apply those years of experience into strong intuitive feelings, and subsequently into good analysis and judgment, you are still considered a novice.

Novices are dangerous. Especially those novices that think they're experts. What is horrifying to your mate is if you talk big game like you're an expert, but your judgments and decision-making are that of recreation-league novice, like "I Got This" Guy. Your intuition is shallow. That's why you second guess yourself. You're indecisive. You don't trust your instincts. But to avoid appearing indecisive, you make hasty judgments based on weak analysis of shallow intuition. And you're wreaking havoc in the lives of the people you're leading.

I know from experience. I used to be one of those fake-me-out experts when I first started working with couples in 2000. I thought I knew everything. After all, I was giving the same advice to my church members that Dr. Phil was giving to people on his television show. Then I came across a couple that showed me I didn't know what I was doing.

They had some extra special issues going on in their marriage. At first, I thought the husband was exaggerating when he told me about some of their issues. Then I thought the wife was just being difficult. I tried to help them, but none of my methods were working. Finally I gave up. They eventually got some professional counseling.

I kept in touch with the husband. He told me that his wife was diagnosed with bipolar disorder. That explains it. I was way out of my depth. Here I thought I was an expert who could help anyone turn their marriage around. But I was proved to be a straight-up novice who didn't know what the heck he was doing. From this experience, I learned what to do when working with clients where someone has an emotional or cognitive disorder. Now I work with a mental health professional that can work with them on an individual basis.

Recommendations for the Novice Decision-Maker

If you are a novice—you know who you are—*do not* follow your intuition…at least until you get some more experience. It will likely be wrong.

If you find the decisions you make are often wrong, rethink how you do your analysis. That's what is failing you. You need to store more information in your long-term memory by learning more.

Just as important, analyze your brain's error messages—those blank emails with no attachments. If you've never seen or heard of something before, then you shouldn't make quick decisions because you don't know what you're doing.

Also, consider heavily the results from your analysis. What are you doing that's working? What are you doing that's not? An empty email with no attachments can tell you a lot about the stimuli itself. If nothing more, it should tell you that if you don't have any experience or feelings about a specific stimulus, then you shouldn't make hasty decisions until you get some more information or advice.

Ask an expert before you make a final decision. If you are embarrassed or don't want anyone to know you don't know what you're doing, here's a little trick I sometimes use: Ask an expert for their input on what you already plan to do. Explain what you're planning, then ask, "From your perspective, is there anything I'm missing?"

This is a confident way to ask for help. You save face because you do have a plan and it also gives the expert a chance to fill in the gaps with their expert advice.

But when they give you advice, don't act like you already knew what they were going to say. From the expert's perspective, that's so irritating. This has happened to me many times. And it frustrated me each time. The next time they ask, I give them a half-hearted response.

Learning from Your Past Feelings and Trusting Them

In the American culture, men are generally socialized to suppress their feelings. Some men have mastered that craft, myself included. If you are a man who is not afraid of your feelings, you don't suppress them, and you know how to interpret them, then you likely make good decisions.

On the other hand, if you are great at suppressing your emotions, avoid understanding how or why your mood fluctuates, or don't take the time to learn what your heart is saying when you have a new feeling you can't explain, then your decisions will likely be sporadic and unstable.

Learn how to understand what your feelings are telling you. Don't suppress them. Embrace them. And learn to trust them. It is only then will you be able to heavily rely on your intuition to make good judgments. And good judgment leads to expert decision-making.

Get extra tips on how to be an expert decision-maker: www.HisLeadershipHerTrust.com/thebook.

Executed Judgment

I can't stress enough how important executing good sound judgment is. Executing judgment is decision-making. And your leadership all boils down to the decisions you make. All this talk about conscious side versus the unconscious side, intuition versus analysis and judgment means nothing to your mate. To her, it's all about the decisions you make.

But for you...

Decision-making isn't just about the decision. It's much deeper than that. It's about your values and your past experiences, and your feelings. It's about how strongly your intuitive feelings influence your decision. It's about how you analyze your intuitive feelings and compare them to all the existing and new stimuli you encounter before making a decision. Then, once you make a decision, it's about being able to initiate roles in your relationship and maintain them.

When there's a problem that needs to be solved or a decision that needs to be made, your mate will look at your judgment and how you executed it to determine if she is willing to trust, respect and follow your leadership in the future. If your judgment is wrong, then the execution of your judgments (your decisions) will be wrong. And the impact will likely be detrimentally felt by one or all within your relationship.

Now I'm not just talking about one incident of poor judgment, but repeated demonstrations of it. A consistent pattern of bad decisions will convince your mate that you don't have good judgment or decision-making. Over time, she will not value the judgment you bring to the relationship.

This diminishes the power resources you bring to the relationship. If your judgment can't be trusted to solve problems, then there will be a power struggle in your relationship over who should make future decisions in that area. And you will lose because your judgment has been proven faulty.

Her negative assessment of your judgment, and the execution thereof, also affects your ability to persuade. You will have difficulty crafting a significant enough argument to persuade her to exchange her confidence in her own BAIB for yours. And if you have no power resources and no ability to persuade, it is impossible for you to provide leadership in that arena.

She may even decide that it's not worth being in a relationship with you anymore because you have become more of a liability than a loving companion. If you find yourself in this place, then you need to take a hard look at how you process information.

If you find it extremely difficult to analyze multiple pieces of information at the same time, get help. Seek out resources. Pride will get you nowhere but confused and alone. And you will forever be getting close to women, only to push them away when they start to see the chinks in your armor of decision-making.

To ensure you can become an expert decision-maker, start at the beginning. Start with your feelings. I don't want to sound cliché, but get in touch with your feelings by working backwards from your behavior to your feelings. Asking your, "What *do* I want to do as a result of what just happened? And why? The answer to "why" will clue you into how you're feeling.

Your feelings will tell you how you should or shouldn't react to stimuli based on your past reactions. The better you can correctly react to stimuli based on your intuitive feelings, the better judgment you will have. Then the execution of your judgments will prove to be a valuable power resource that is used to the benefit of your relationship.

Chapter 10:
Step 4: Check-In...Often

"Checking in" is essentially checking with your mate to see how things are going. This is the easiest step among the four. But because it's so easy, it's often overlooked.

If you fail to check in with your mate during the execution step, a serious flaw might exist with your decision and you won't know it until it's too late. You then risk losing the confidence, trust, and respect of your mate because she doesn't feel you are capable of handling the situation. And those feelings get stored in her Department of Archives and will be used to intuitively influence her decision whether to follow you in the future or not.

Checking-in is similar to 'communicate and wait'. When you execute your judgment, you are communicating to her through your decisions and how you carry them out. Your mate looks at these actions and makes a determination if your judgment is sound or not.

You need to know what she's thinking to determine how well or horribly you're doing. Proactively check-in with her to find out if everything is going according to plan.

If it's not, don't get upset, get an attitude, or shut down. Use that new information to re-analyze the situation and modify your approach as necessary. Then execute your judgment again.

Learn to adapt and adjust to life as it happens. You might have to analyze and make modifications to your judgment several times until you get it right. So build extra time into your planning to account for adjustments and adaptations.

If none occur, then you'll get credited for solving the problem faster than expected and gain favor in the eyes of your mate. She will then be more likely to trust you, respect you, and actually want to follow your leadership in the future.

Follow this same iterative process until the problem is solved or the task is accomplished.

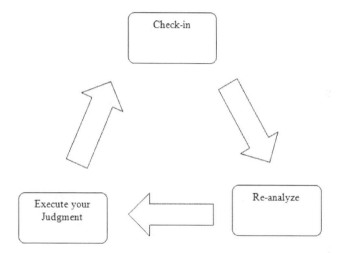

Chapter 11:
Conclusion

Need help obtaining or maintaining leadership in your relationship? Get personal one-on-one coaching with Heath: www.HisLeadershipHerTrust.com/thebook.

Personally Speaking

My quest to understand leadership was a long road. And it was a difficult one, too. As a young man in my early 20s, I always knew that I wanted to have a happy marriage with just one woman. I didn't want to get divorced. So I put a lot of emphasis on trying to figure out how to pick the best person for me. So I searched high and low, wide and deep for Mrs. Right. I had a long list of criteria Mrs. Right had to meet. And I wasn't settling.

However, during my search I realized that no matter whom I picked and whatever qualities she had, I would inevitably screw up my marriage because of who *I* was. See, I got my heart broken by some chick in high school. I was hurt so bad that I vowed that I would never feel that way again. So I protected my feelings. I became selfish, stingy, arrogant, sarcastic, insensitive, and uncaring—just to name a few. I presented that version of Heath Wiggins to the world over the next 10 years.

This wasn't the Heath Wiggins God created me to be. This was not the Heath Wiggins who would be able to initiate and maintain a marriage. I knew I had to change. If I was ever going to get married, I had to grow up overcome my issues of self-esteem and rejection or else my marriage would fail.

I started going to church and my values began to change. My outlook on women, relationships, and life itself started changing. I started caring about women's feelings. My behavior improved too. I changed my communication patterns so I wouldn't come off so abrasive. I began encouraging people. And the biggest change was I began giving money to friends in need.

Some of my friends didn't believe this transformation was real. They thought it was just a fad and I would return back to the Heath of old. It took about 18 months before I felt I had a grasp of the new and improved Heath Wiggins. I knew I didn't have all the answers, but I was confident with the answers I had. I felt it was safe for me to move to the next step—to get me a wife.

Bernie and I married in October 1997. Because I prepared beforehand, we started out strong. We were able to easily resolve the problems every young married couple experiences. But after a few short years, I reached the threshold that my preparation provided. I knew I needed to up my game. As a husband—the appointed leader of my family—I felt woefully inept to lead. I needed to know how to make those serious decisions that a husband should make, the kind that benefit the family and not harm it.

Unfortunately, the mentors I had were primarily teaching me from their experiences. The problem with that was I felt like they were trying to teach me how to be like them. I would often hear my mentors tell me, "Well, if it were me, I'd do XYZ..." Or, "This is what I didn't do in this situation..."

Their advice was much appreciated. But their background, experiences, and value systems were much different than mine. I didn't always agree with their recommendations. Sometimes their opinions and recommendations felt foreign to me.

I felt like I was literally just flubbing my way through life…a true novice. And this wasn't the way to lead. This ultimately was the catalyst that prodded me to start learning about how to lead and how to make better decisions.

What I ultimately learned was that my Christian faith defines who I am and what I believe, but so do my past experiences. The totality of my life experiences created my beliefs and value system. These past experiences also subconsciously anchor my feelings and serve as a point of reference for current and future experiences.

And it's those feelings that give me perspective when I'm deciding how I'm going to initiate roles in my relationship, how to use my power resources to communicate a persuasive message to my wife and wait for her feedback, and how to execute my judgment and make decisions beneficial to our family.

Likewise, your feelings are center stage of your understanding. How you felt prescribes how you'll feel. And how you feel influences your judgment and decisions.

Next Steps

You have the same challenges of leadership I have. Whether you're male or female, married or single, dating or engaged, we're all faced with the same leadership challenges, albeit in different ways.

Here are some recommendations for both men and women—married, dating, or single alike. Let's start with the men.

Men

Let's start with your purpose—the reason why you were created is to fill, subdue, and rule. Be clear on this: whatever you do in life will ultimately fall into those three categories. Whether it's a life-long problem you're supposed to confront, like Martin Luther King Jr. did for civil rights; or a life-long goal you're supposed to accomplish, like Barack Obama did in seeking to become the first African-American president.

But the truth is, sometimes the quest to control your own destiny and forge your own way seems less scary than following the path God created for you. It also requires less patience because you don't have to wait on God, or go through the tests and trials of many kinds that He strategically places in your path. I definitely understand that.

But you will ultimately end up doing what God wants you to do anyway. For Proverbs 16:9 informs us of this difficult but true fact: "*In his heart a man plans his course, but the LORD determines his steps.*"

The good news is that God gives you the ability to do exactly what He assigned you to do: "*All these are the work of one and the same Spirit, and he gives them to each one, just as He determines.*" (1 Corinthians 12:11). So don't be intimidated by God's seemingly insurmountable challenges nor shun His process for overcoming them. And at the end of those trials, you will see perseverance develop into maturity in all its grandeur. You won't lack anything you need to pursue what God has assigned you to accomplish.

By being tested this way, instead of your preferred no-trials way, you will learn what God wants you to do, how to do it, and when to do it.

Until this awakening comes, practice the I.C.E.C. leadership steps on various task-oriented goals in multiple areas of your life. This is the best way for you to learn how

269

to provide leadership and become an expert decision maker. Practice. Practice. Practice.

Learn to rely on your his intuition rather than his analysis. Continue storing leadership experiences in your Department of Archives. The more the merrier. The stronger your intuition, the better your judgment and decision-making.

Throw yourself into as many opportunities to provide leadership as possible. Don't be afraid to do it. Or, be afraid to do it and do it anyway. Start putting yourself out there and provide leadership in any organizationally structured activity/relationship you can. This is the best way to become an expert decision-maker and leader in relationships. To this there is no substitute, shortcut, or work around. You must start practicing leadership to perfect it.

Four-Part Challenge for Existing Male Leaders

If you are already doing this or are already a leader in an organization, I have a challenge for you. Observe your process of influence. It has four parts.

1. Identify how you use your power resources to control TRIPAR in your organization. Take note of anything you want to improve.

2. Observe how you communicate persuasive messages to lead or change someone's BAIB. Again, take note of anything you want to improve.

3. Observe how you analyze your intuition and arrive at a judgment. All this information serves as your baseline for how you currently provide leadership. Take one to three weeks to observe these three attributes of leadership. Write down your baseline so you won't have to try and remember it when you revisit it later.

4. Over the next three months, make the desired improvements for how you use your power resources to control TRIPAR and how you craft your persuasive communications to change one's BAIB. At the end of three months, compare the same leadership capabilities against your baseline. Take note of any changes in how you analyze your intuition and arrive at judgments. Take note of how your leadership has improved. Document the changes. This is your new baseline.

Repeat this process every three months for at least a year. You should immediately notice significant changes in your leadership ability. Your intuition will be sharper. Your judgment will be more sound. Your mate will respond more positively to you because you use your power resources purposefully. You will communicate more clearly. And you will make decisions quicker and more accurately.

Single Men

Get in as much practice providing leadership in organizations or relationships where there are problems to solve or task-oriented goals. You aren't in a committed relationship for which these leadership skills must come to fruition yet. So you have time to perfect your game.

Then, try it out on some willing, yet unsuspecting young lady. And once you execute these changes, she will be blown away at how tight and put together you are. To her, you will be a breath of fresh air. Follow these three steps to improve your leadership:

5. Learn by observing what these leaders do right and wrong. Observe how they use their power resources to control TRIPAR. Observe how they communicate

persuasive messages and how they sway the confidence of others to change their BAIB. Keep what you deem valuable. Discard what you don't. You are building up your leadership arsenal of power resources.

6. Look for a wide variety of task-oriented projects and problems to solve that have varying degrees of complexity. Carefully walk through the I.C.E.C. leadership model step by step. Monitor your progress as you go. Keep track of which power resources work and which don't. Analyze how you use your intuition and analysis to arrive at your judgment.

7. Create a baseline of how you make your judgments after you check-in with the members of your organization. Assess how you used your power resources and persuasive communication efforts. Were they effective? Did it work? Each time you check-in, assess the same factors. Assess how heavily you relied on your intuition versus your analysis. Make adjustments where necessary.

The more you check-in with your members, the better judgment you will have. So get in as much practice as you can. The better judgment you have, the more desirable women will find you, because they trust and respect your judgment. Good judgment is attractive because it's associated with a women's need for security in a relationship. To her, it means she can trust you to make good decisions with her best interest in mind and not do something completely ignorant and stupid.

Dating Men

Leadership Only Exists in an Organization

If you are already in a committed relationship, do all the things I told the single men to do. Do *not*, I repeat, *do not* try to use the I.C.E.C. leadership process in your relationship *unless* you're in a relationship that is structured like an organization. If your relationship is structured like a group, no leadership exists in your relationship.

However, there might be some task-oriented activities that the two of you do together where leadership is involved, like helping each other solve a problem or plan an event. Use those opportunities to practice your leadership skills. See if she is someone you want to create some common goals with. See where it leads.

Upgrading to an Organizationally Structured Relationship

If you want to take your relationship to an organizationally structured relationship, identify a common purpose-oriented goal you both want to pursue in your relationship, like wanting to seek pre-marital counseling. Use the I.C.E.C. leadership model to pursue it. Initiate the roles. Then communicate and wait for her feedback. Next, execute your judgment and check-in with her to see how everything is going. Make adjustments as necessary.

Married or Engaged Men

Structure Your Relationship Like an Organization

For my married or engaged men, your instructions are a little different. I don't distinguish between married and being engaged from a leadership standpoint, because the man who's engaged should be practicing what he's going to do when he gets married. So you two gentlemen are grouped together.

In this group, there may be varying relational statuses. One man may be married, but his relationship is structured like a group. Another may be engaged, but his relationship is structured like an organization…and vice versa.

Identify a Problem that Needs to be Solved or a Common Goal

Regardless of where your relationship status, identify a problems that needs to be solved or find a common goal for the relationship to pursue. In that pursuit, each person should have different roles and responsibilities. Now you can start providing leadership.

Warning: Sometimes men like to go hard or go home. Do *not* take on the largest, biggest, most longstanding, and difficult issue in your relationship. I don't have anything against you personally, and I'm not suggesting you will fail. But it has been my experience that starting smaller projects and building momentum builds confidence and expertise in tackling larger ones in the future. Plus, if you happen to fail at your first attempt, the impact won't be so big because the issue/problem wasn't so significant.

But if you go big and fail, your failure will be stored in *her* Department of Archives and be recalled every time you try to lead in the near future. Additionally, you will have lost her confidence, making it very difficult for you to try to persuade her to follow you next time. So my recommendation is to start off small and build your confidence and momentum for future endeavors.

As you continue, success and failure will be your friends. Both of these experiences are being stored in your Department of Archives for future reference. So in the future when you encounter similar stimuli, your intuition will be stronger. With strong judgment, your decisions will be quicker and more accurate, improving your leadership skills at every turn. And that's how your mate will ultimately judge your leadership skills, by how you execute your judgment in making decisions.

Women

I didn't forget about the ladies. I'm not leaving you out. I know there are some single, dating, engaged, and married women who want to know what they should do while these men get their leadership game up. Here's what you need to do.

Single and Dating Women

Practice and hone your skills as a facilitator. These skills of a facilitator are directly keeping with your purpose as a woman. A facilitator makes things happen. She adds value to everything she touches. You will add great value to your relationship because you possess tremendous power resources that can be used to enhance any relationship you are in, currently or in the future.

A woman with great facilitator skills has the capability to become a great leader too. Leadership is not person-specific. So the greater leadership skills you have, the more efficient and productive your relationship will be at solving problems and accomplishing task-oriented goals.

It will require any male prospect you are dating, or will consider dating in the future, to bring his A-game if he wants to get serious with you and approach that organizational relationship status. This is beneficial because the ones that can't hang will self-destruct right before your eyes.

Work in a variety of professional organizations so you can be exposed to different types of leadership. The more diverse the better. You'll learn what type of leadership suits you. You'll also learn how to assess someone's judgment objectively, without the haze of bias brought on by emotional feelings that sometimes clouds judgment. This way you'll know what type of leadership works best for you. And you'll notice it in a man in the future.

This will also give you a chance to understand how you serve. Understanding how you serve in different organizational settings will heighten your awareness of your strengths and weaknesses. It's best to learn the kind of leadership you can serve under in a non-dating relationship. And through your service, you will learn how to spot the kind of leadership that's acceptable to you. You won't be fooled by the smoke and mirrors cast by those lackluster men who know how to run game. Your intuitive judgment will reveal them for the frauds they are.

Married and Engaged Women

Just like the men, I grouped the married and engaged women into the same category. Their common goal is the same, to live happily ever after with their mate. The difference is, the engaged woman is still in preparation mode, while the married woman is in implementation mode.

As I said earlier, women are not stupid. They have their own beliefs, thoughts, and ideas. They also have their own God-given skills, abilities, and gifts. They come to a relationship with their own power resources. And they know how to use them.

So to the married and engaged women, I say use them to the fullest. Use them to help your mate solve problems and accomplish task-oriented goals. Use them to help him lead.

Even though the role of leadership in a marriage has been assigned to the man, your intuitive leadership skills can help him by providing wise counsel and leadership to certain areas of the relationship.

Your assignment is to deploy your gifts, skills, and abilities in whatever way necessary to help him accomplish the common goal set before you.

Some of you may be thinking, "What if my man doesn't know how to lead?" Well duh! Your first step is to get him this book. I wish you all the best.

God bless!

References

Bass, B. M., & Bass, R. (2008). *The Bass Handbook of Leadership: Theory, Research, & Managerial Applications.* New York: Free Press.

Brunner, B., & Rowen, B. (n.d.). *The Equal Pay Act: A History of Pay Inequity in the U.S.* Retrieved 11 21, 2014, from http://www.infoplease.com/: http://www.infoplease.com/spot/equalpayact1.html

Campitelli, G., & Gobet, F. (2010). Herbert Simon's decision-making approach: Investigation of cognitive processes in experts. *Review of General Psychology, 14* (4), 354-364.

Cherlin, A. (1992). *Marriage, Divorce, Remarriage.* United States of America: the Presidents and Fellow at Harvard College.

Dreyfus, S., & Dreyfus, H. (1980, 02). *A five stage model of the mental activities involved in directed skill acquisition.* Retrieved April 01, 2014, from Defense Technical Information Center:

http://www.dtic.mil/cgi-
bin/GetTRDoc?AD=ADA084551

French, J., & Raven, B. (1959). The Basis of Power. In D.
C. (Ed), *Studies in Social Power* (pp. 259-269). Ann
Arbor: University of Michigan Press.

Gibbs, N. (2009, 10 14). *The State of the American Woman.*
Retrieved 05 27, 2011, from Time.com:
http://content.time.com/time/specials/packages/artic
le/0,28804,1930277_1930145_1930309-2,00.html

Hemphill, J. (1949). Situational factors in leadership. *Ohio
State University. Bureau of Educational Research
Monograph , 32,* 136.

Homans, G. (1947). A conceptual scheme for the study of
social organization. *American Sociological Review ,
12,* 13-26.

Hovland, C., Janis, I., & Kelley, H. (1953). *Communication
and persuasion: psychological studies of opinion
change.* New Haven: Yale University Press.

Jaccard, J. (1981). Toward Theories of Persuasion and Belief Change. *Journal of Personality and Social Psychology*, *40* (2), 260-269.

Kahneman, D., & Tversky, A. (1979). Prospect theory: An analysis of decision under risk. *Econometrica: Journal of the Econometric Society*, 263-291.

Lehrer, J. (2009). *How we decide.* New York: Houghton Mifflin Harcourt.

Maslow, A. (1943). A Theory of Human Motivation. *Psychological Reveiw*, *50*, 370-396.

National Marriage Project and the Institute for American Values. (2012, December). The State of Our Unions Marriage in America 2012. Charlottesville, VA, US.

Reynolds, S. (2006). A neurocognitive model of the ethical decision-making process: implications for study and practice. *Journal of Applied Psychology*, *91* (4), 737-748.

Rogerson, M., Gottlieb, M., Handelsman, M., Knapp, S., & Younggren, J. (2011). Nonrational processes in ethical decision making. *American Psychologist , 66* (7), 614-623.

Stogdill, R. (1959). *Individual behavior and group achievement.* New York: Oxford University Press.

Stogdill, R. (1950). Leadership, Membership, and Organization. *Psychological Bulletin , 47* (1), 1-14.

Tay, L., & Deiner, E. (2011). Needs and Subjective Well-Being Around the World . *Journal of Personality and Social Psychology , 101* (2), 354–365.

The Yale Center for Dyslexia & Creativity. (n.d.). *Multicultural Dyslexia Awareness Initiative.* Retrieved 11 2014, from The Yale Center for Dyslexia & Creativity: http://dyslexia.yale.edu/MDAI/

Tuckman, B. (1965). Developmental sequence in small groups. *Psychological Bulletin , 63,* 384-399.

U.S. Census Bureau . (2011, 11). *America's Families and Living Arrangements: 2011.* Retrieved 03 04, 2013, from https://www.census.gov:

https://www.census.gov/hhes/families/data/cps2011
.html

Walvoord, J., & Zuck, R. (1983). *The Bible Knowledge Commentary: New Testament.* Colorado Springs: Zondervan Publishing House.

Warner, Lee, & Lee. (1986). Social Organization, Spousal Resources, and Marital Power: A cross-cultural Study. *Journals of Marriage and the Family , 48*, 121-128.

Znaniecki, F. (1945). Social organization and institutions. In G. Gurvitch, & W. E. Moore, *Twentieth Century Sociology* (pp. 172-217). New York: Philosophical Library.